Street, Palace, Square

JAN-WERNER MÜLLER

Street, Palace, Square

The Architecture of Democratic Spaces

ALLEN LANE
an imprint of
PENGUIN BOOKS

ALLEN LANE

UK | USA | Canada | Ireland | Australia
India | New Zealand | South Africa

Allen Lane is part of the Penguin Random House group of companies
whose addresses can be found at global.penguinrandomhouse.com.

Penguin Random House UK
One Embassy Gardens, 8 Viaduct Gardens, London SW11 7BW

penguin.co.uk

Penguin
Random House
UK

First published in Great Britain by Allen Lane 2026

001

Copyright © Jan-Werner Müller, 2026

Set in 12.1/15.2pt Dante MT Std
Typeset by Six Red Marbles UK, Thetford, Norfolk
Printed and bound in Great Britain by Clays Ltd, Elcograf S.p.A.

The authorized representative in the EEA is Penguin Random House Ireland,
Morrison Chambers, 32 Nassau Street, Dublin D02 YH68

A CIP catalogue record for this book is available from the British Library

ISBN: 978-0-241-38203-5

To the memory of
László Rajk (1949–2019)

Contents

Introduction: The Building that Brought Democracy

Taxi drivers no less than politicians can be heard saying: 'He brought us democracy'.[1] They are not referring to a great constitution-maker or hero of national liberation; they are invoking an architect, and a foreign one to boot: the American Louis Kahn, who designed the parliament building in Dhaka during the 1960s, in what was then East Pakistan. In 1971 construction had to be paused during the Bangladesh War of Independence between March and December, at which point the country gained its sovereignty. Kahn died in 1974; the parliament building was completed only in 1982. Kahn's edifice not only came to symbolize democracy; rather, it appears to some at least as an actor in and even *for* democracy. As the Bangladeshi architect Shamsul Wares, who at one time worked under Kahn, enthused: 'When parliament was out of session, the building stood like our conscience, watching us, waiting for us to do the right thing'.[2]

When I went to Dhaka in spring 2025, many Bangladeshis thought they had done the right thing: the year before they had driven the country's authoritarian ruler, Sheikh Hasina, daughter of the country's founding president, Sheikh Mujibur Rahman, into exile in India. The building – officially the Jatiya Sangsad Bhaban – continued to stand, and maybe

A Citadel for Democracy? Louis Kahn's parliament in Dhaka.

still functioned like a conscience. Its inside had been badly damaged, though, so much so that the chamber of deputies was off limits to the foreign visitor. A security guard on the vast brick plaza in front of the parliament recounted the 'storming' of the building in 2024 and explained that bodies had been floating in the water which surrounds what Kahn had called a 'citadel' for assembly. I wondered whether people had taken their political anger out on the building. What was the meaning of attacking a country's supposed political conscience?

A 'storming' of what is supposed to be the 'people's house' has not just shocked observers in south-east Asia in recent years: other examples have been the Capitol in Washington, DC, on 6 January 2021; federal government buildings in Brasília, on 8 January 2023. Also, harmless by comparison and half-forgotten: the attempt by an agitated crowd to enter the Berlin Reichstag in late August 2020, which was held off, in the end, by two policemen wielding nothing but batons.

As it happens, within sight of the Reichstag stands a building inspired by Kahn's work: Germany's 'new' Chancellery, completed in 2001. The large round openings of its boxy concrete facade – very similar to what can be seen in Dhaka – were to serve as 'stargates of the political imagination', or so the architect, Axel Schultes, claimed; Germans, more prosaically, often refer to the world's largest executive building as 'the washing machine'.[3]

Few tend to see this edifice as particularly democratic. Schultes himself has complained that something crucial is missing. He and his business partner Charlotte Frank had been chosen personally by the then head of government, Helmut Kohl, after the decision to move the capital from Bonn to Berlin.[4] For the space between the Chancellery and a large building for parliamentary offices Schultes and Frank had designed a 'civic forum'. Today, there is no such thing; instead, one finds just empty, desolate, one might even say dead space; space that is also subject to severe restrictions on political protest.

The issue is not just that politicians fail to deliver what architects (not to mention the people) want. One also wonders what a 'forum' – a word and an idea going back to the ancient Roman Republic, implying a multiplicity of uses beyond politics – would have really meant in a large contemporary nation state. How might it have redeemed the promise of 'democratic architecture' which many politicians had made when designs for the post-Cold War capital were being considered in the 1990s?

Schultes and Frank did not only get to build the Chancellery. Their master plan for the whole area around the parliament was also chosen partly because they had proposed an axis of edifices crossing the area where the Berlin Wall had once stood. This Federal Ribbon stretching from east to west, jumping over the river Spree twice, was meant not merely to signal a symbolic overcoming of the division of the two Germanies; it was also intended as a rebuke to one of the twentieth century's most infamous urban plans: Hitler had sought to replace Berlin with a new capital, 'Germania'; it would have featured a gigantic north-south axis, a *via triumphalis* that the Führer insisted had to be wider than the Champs-Elysées.

Had there been something inherently *undemocratic* about the design by Albert Speer, Hitler's chief architect? Axes used to be associated with royal power; but they feature even in brand-new capitals of countries wishing to be seen as anything but monarchies: think of Washington, DC, or Brasília. Capitals are replaced surprisingly often: just in recent years, there is Egypt's 'New Administrative Capital' fifty kilometres east of Cairo and inaugurated in 2024 (the city does not have its own name yet); there is Naypyidaw, the military's administrative capital for Myanmar created in 2005, far away from any potentially unruly urban masses; and there is Indonesia's Nusantara, a capital still under construction, replacing Jakarta, which is slowly sinking into the sea. When governments can build on a tabula rasa, they want to find ways to signal a commitment to democracy, even if the political reality, as in Egypt and Myanmar, is deeply authoritarian. Might the specifics of individual edifices or of urban spaces indicate whether a promise of democracy is real or not? Can buildings lie?

An extraordinary test case is a brand-new futuristic city in Saudi Arabia's north-west. Dubbed The Line, it is, well, a line, which is to say: a linear city. It will supposedly be one long building stretching 170 kilometres when completed, in essence one giant structure consisting of two skyscrapers 500 metres high, separated by 200 metres from each other, with an intended population density ten times that of Manhattan. This corridor of mirroring facades is part of a grand plan for developing the region of 'Neom' – the name a forced merger between *neos* and *mustaqbal*, the Arabic for 'future'.[5] The Line is being touted by its chief promoter, Crown Prince Mohamad bin Salman, as environmentally friendly; unlike conventional, sprawling cities, it is said to leave nature alone. Supposedly, there will be no cars, but an underground high-speed train running beneath the entire city, which, like Egypt's New Administrative Capital, is touted to be 'smart'.

According to a stunning exhibition in Venice's Abbazia di San Gregorio – one of the most amazing among many amazing edifices overlooking the Grand Canal – The Line will also offer what the curators called 'ubiquitous public realm' (sic!). Public space almost always comes up when people talk about architecture and democracy. But can a linear city truly offer such space? Just what might be missing in this megastructure in the desert if it ever gets built: at the time of writing, work has stopped and the future of the project is in serious doubt – other than the basic political freedoms already missing in the kingdom?

Taking up such questions, this book explores the relationship between democracy on the one hand and, on the other, architecture and urbanism. That there is such a relationship is not obvious to everyone: Helmut Kohl's very own minister for housing once denied outright that there could be such a thing as 'democratic architecture'; at the same time, he insisted, somewhat paradoxically, that 'bad architecture can never count as democratic'.[6] To be sure, there is a long history of architects declaring specific buildings and spaces indubitably 'democratic'. Frank Lloyd Wright liberally dispensed pronouncements about architecture and democracy over the course of his long career; at one point he asserted that 'a democratic building is at ease; it stands relaxed. A democratic building . . . is for and belongs to the people. It is of human scale for men and women to live in and feel at home'. Minoru Yamasaki, architect of the Twin Towers in New York, echoed his American colleague when he called for 'designing buildings as relaxed, friendly, and enjoyable places, the very qualities of the democracy we hold dear'.[7] More recently, Daniel Libeskind, responsible for the master plan for Ground Zero and a 'Freedom Tower' meant to replace the fallen Towers (his proposal was never implemented), claimed that the process of finding a design for the devastated area in Lower Manhattan had been a truly democratic experience. He also congratulated himself for having created 'a space for people, not just corporations'.[8]

It is easy to dismiss such pronouncements as mere public relations. After all, architects do not simply sell designs; they sell designs with and through a story. At a time when democracy is globally under threat – but still the most sought-after political designation (even the leaders of Azerbaijan and Russia want to be called democrats) – linking ideas for buildings with some vague appeal to democratic values is an obvious marketing strategy. As cities find themselves under pressure to attract ever more tourists by means of 'iconic' edifices, it also makes sense for architects to deliver uplifting narratives about liberty, equality or, for that matter, 'ubiquitous public realm' which will sound good and make everyone feel good. As Bjarke Ingels, the brilliant, ever-enthusiastic Danish architect, once put it: 'I really like this idea that architecture is the art and science of trying to make everybody happy'.[9] Happiness, democracy . . . it seems anything and everything can be attached to architectural spectacles.

We should pay less attention to what architects, 'starchitects' in particular, say, and more to what their designs tell us.[10] With or without PR brochures, the built environment must be understood as necessarily political, for it reflects relationships of power and also has consequences for such relationships. True, in one sense, building is inevitable – humans have always needed shelter – but this inevitability does not make architecture apolitical in the way the weather could be said to be apolitical (at least until we belatedly woke up to our conduct's effects on climate).[11]

Creating shelter is usually a collective endeavour. But who gets to design and who comes to command others to build? It takes power, in the sense of capacity, but also authority, in the sense of getting others to obey, in order to create the built environment: Le Corbusier's book *La Ville radieuse* (*Radiant City*) began with a bold 'This work is dedicated to AUTHORITY'. Aristotle intimated that architects might have special insights into the operation of power: in his *Politics* he observed that the architect and urban planner Hippodamus of Miletus – responsible for the street plan of Piraeus, an early version of the grid – was 'the first person, not actually engaged in politics, to attempt to say something about the best constitution'.[12]

Building requires power; once created, our environment structures how we relate to each other. Winston Churchill, apropos the debate about how to reconstruct the House of Commons after the Luftwaffe had dropped two incendiary bombs on it in 1941, remarked: 'first we shape our buildings, and then our buildings shape us'.[13] But how so? On the most basic level, the built environment includes and excludes; it can make some people visible and others invisible. It also enables and constrains people to act in particular ways:[14] a wall cuts off an African-American neighbourhood from a white one; bridges have been designed so low that buses cannot pass under them (keeping those who depend on public transportation from going to particular places).[15] Buildings make us move in certain ways, especially when people are around who might push us further along and assign particular places to us. The Danish theorist Steen Eiler Rasmussen observed apropos one of the world's most famous (and most imitated) edifices, the Palace of Versailles, that it featured 'dynamic spatial planning with rhythmical series of rooms in which none is treated as an independent unit'. These, he argued, were 'entirely in keeping with the whole system of Absolutism', for the royal residence 'was formed like an eel trap, that is to say, all movement went in one direction only, each room opening on to another and all leading to a symbol of the regime: a royal statue, a throne room, or an audience chamber presided over by the all-powerful king himself. Though Baroque layouts were not . . . used for processions, they were designed as though they were'.[16] The dramaturgy of absolutism consisted of inevitable movement towards the king, the centre of it all.[17]

But architecture clearly isn't all about coercion. Hannah Arendt observed that 'before men began to act, a definite space had to be secured and a structure built where all subsequent actions could take place' – suggesting that constraints, even walls, are not always denying freedom, but means to create clearly delimited space for political action.[18] Buildings also enable.

Friedrich Nietzsche held that, in buildings, the will to power becomes visible; he also asserted that 'the most powerful' have always inspired architects. But, in his eyes, architecture wasn't only about commanding: he also wrote that it could flatter and even 'persuade'.[19] A contemporary of Nietzsche, Victor Hugo, inserted a curious theoretical treatise on architecture in the middle of his novel *The Hunchback of Notre Dame*.[20] In a chapter entitled 'This Will Kill That' he claimed that, for centuries, humanity had expressed its thoughts in stone: buildings had given ideas permanence; they had communicated the essence of particular ages. What supposedly 'killed' this form of self-expression? The printing press. Now people could record thoughts on paper; and they were able to achieve a far wider circulation of ideas, a possibility that, according to Hugo, lent the world created by Gutenberg a much more 'popular' character.

Yet the function of architecture to record and inculcate thought, including political thought, did not disappear. In fact, Hugo's term *la pensée écrite en pierre* – thought written in stone – reappeared almost literally in an expression often used by National Socialist functionaries: *Wort aus Stein*. Hitler himself mused that 'the stones really speak, when human beings are silent'.[21] However one conceives of such 'speech' – it does not constrain in the way walls would. Rather, it might *cue* us one way or another: it makes us think of something; it reminds us of something; it might put us in a particular mood.[22]

Plenty of buildings – especially but not only government buildings – offer political messages: they are popular media, just like newspapers are media; unlike the latter, they are often in our face, whether we like it or not.[23] Yet, for the most part, we are not receptive to the message: we don't look up at buildings as we walk; instead, we look down at screens. That kind of inattention is hardly new: already by the 1930s, Walter Benjamin observed that the built environment is usually experienced in a state of distraction.[24] Building is a basic human necessity; contemplating buildings is not. To be sure, we inevitably relate to architecture in both an optical and, less obviously, a haptic manner – it is impossible not to see, and, when it comes to shelter, impossible not to touch, the built environment. But it is perfectly possible never truly to think about architecture, including anything political its designers might have wished to communicate. Political regimes have always used it for political messaging; but the most effective use can be via cues received in everyday situations when we are not concentrating on our environment at all – just as the most effective way for ideologies to be reproduced is the unthinking repetition of seemingly commonsensical ideas everyone takes for granted.

Is buildings messaging us directly, so to speak, primarily a matter of distinct styles, or perhaps recognizably democratic icons? Some of the creators of modern democracy certainly thought so: the most radical French revolutionaries erected statues of Hercules, based on the idea that he was strong, and so were the people. But the image proved illegible to the people themselves, even when a leader instructed them 'that giant is you!'[25] Some eminent political practitioners no less than philosophers think there's a reason for that illegibility:

democracy is said to be uniquely abstract; it's about processes, not about people or things. In 1831, two years after his term ended, the sixth American president, John Quincy Adams, held that 'democracy has no monuments. It strikes no medals; it bears the head of no man upon its coin; its very essence is iconoclastic'. Never mind that we have statues of Washington, Churchill, even a Goddess of Democracy created by students on Tiananmen Square in the spring of 1989, and never mind that the world's tallest statue is not in North Korea, but was erected in the largest democracy ever to have existed: the Statue of Unity (182 metres high), a likeness of the anti-colonial hero Sardar Patel, to be found in Narendra Modi's home state of Gujarat.[26]

My aim here is to make us more conscious of the politics of architecture, and the relationship between the built environment and democracy in particular. How should we imagine a distinctly democratic built environment? Would it just have to be the outcome of political processes in which as many citizens as possible can decide about design? Or should the primary issues be how architecture and urban spaces can best represent democracy *to* citizens – and how architecture and city planning can concretely facilitate democratic action *by* citizens?

In answering these questions, we have to engage the question whether democracy suffers from something like an 'iconographic deficit'. But the main focus of our inquiry will be on spaces, both outside and inside edifices.[27] These can represent and facilitate democracy. They cannot guarantee it, obviously. Yet talk about architecture and politics is pervaded by what one might call spatial determinism: certain spaces, or so we are told, will reliably produce certain outcomes. Jeremy

Bentham, the utilitarian social reformer, was a great believer in this sort of thing; apropos his panopticon, he rejoiced: 'Morals reformed – health preserved – industry invigorated – instruction diffused – public burthen lightened – Economy seated as it were upon a rock – the Gordian knot of the Poor Laws not cut but untied – all by a simple idea in Architecture'.[28]

Spatial determinists fail to see how laws matter for what happens in particular spaces: an open public square does not guarantee a public sphere, that is to say, a shared world of arguing about politics. China boasts the world's largest square, in the southern port city of Dalian; it also boasts what is arguably the world's most tightly controlled square, Tiananmen.[29]

The law is not the only relevant variable missing from many discussions of architecture and democracy; we must also look very carefully at what I have called cuing: suggesting some behaviour as appropriate and some as not. Contrary to plenty of kitschy communitarian stories, even the nicest park will not magically make for random encounters through which citizens learn about diverse political perspectives that other members of the polity hold. Come to think of it: when and where was the last time one had chance conversations anywhere? The most likely answer today is 'on the internet!'

Resisting determinism and simplistic stories about rendering abstract political principles in three dimensions is not endorsing 'anything goes' relativism.[30] As the Italian architect Aldo Rossi (who started his career as a Communist and ended up designing for Disney in Florida) once put it: the architect can set the table, the meal is another matter.[31] There is still plenty to be said about the table – and, by implication, about the edifices and spaces people need, given what they want to do in a democracy and where they might plausibly do it.

On occasion, our question can be illuminated by stark contrasts; that is why I shall also turn to examining building strategies pursued by authoritarian regimes. Many of the contemporary ones are subtle; autocrats are careful not to remind both domestic and international audiences of any totalitarian aesthetics of the twentieth century. But the latter's actual history itself is more complicated than usually thought; not every fascist building looked like the stereotypical gigantic classical edifices intended for Speer's Germania.

Bringing architecture and democracy together might have an unexpected benefit: as we shuttle back and forth between reflections on spaces, styles, and symbols on the one hand and theories of democracy on the other, perhaps we will see something about democracy that we did not see before. We'll have a first go at this in the next chapter, in which I shall revisit the ancient world in order to argue that democracy always needs two sites – literally – to function: on the one hand, a place for formal, collectively binding decision-making, and, on the other hand, a space, or, for that matter, multiple spaces, that enable the informal creation of political views.[32] Squares are a prime example, but, as we shall see later in the book, there are also forms of democratic politics for which streets are better suited.

Spaces and particular buildings might not bring us democracy in the way Louis Kahn's parliament is supposed to have done – but analysing them might bring us to a deeper understanding of what we want and can expect from democracy.

Square: Uses of Assembly

I can take any empty space and call it a bare stage. A man walks across this empty space whilst someone else is watching him, and this is all that is needed for an act of theatre to be engaged.

Peter Brook

When one allows a political association to place centres of action at certain points of the country, its activity becomes greater and its influence more extended. There men see each other; means of execution are combined and opinions are deployed with the force and heat that written thought can never attain.

Alexis de Tocqueville, *Democracy in America*

In the beginning there was an empty space. Or so ancient historians tell us: in Greece an agora required no specific buildings but simply markers designating it as a space for assembly – and for business.[1] It was not the only distinctly public space: there were sacred sites honouring various deities, and the necropolis, the place for the dead.[2] Rival political systems featured such spaces as well. But only the Greek polis created an open public place for political argument, for juries staffed by citizens, and for civic rituals like ostracism.

Open space, a stage for the people? That very image,

throughout the history of social and political thought, has tended to conjure up anxieties. Consider James Madison: 'In all very numerous assemblies, of whatever characters composed, passion never fails to wrest the sceptre from reason. Had every Athenian citizen been a Socrates; every Athenian assembly would still have been a mob'.[3] One does not have to be a more or less conservative American founding father to voice such concerns about assemblies. James Baldwin held that 'anyone who has ever been at the mercy of the people . . . knows something awful about us . . . and avoids even the most convivial of mobs'.[4]

Will we find out more about 'us' – and our propensity to form 'mobs' – if we go back to Athens and Rome?[5] Leaps back into ancient times might be scintillating but what we bring back from such excursions often appears pitifully naive, since it's so ahistorical. True, we still call all kinds of spaces, physical and metaphorical, 'agora'.[6] But do we have any sense of what those concepts meant originally? For instance, can we even remotely fathom that practices we may superficially read as 'democratic' in Athens or as 'republican' in Rome were embedded in a world of religious cults, many of which make absolutely no sense to us? Political gatherings and decisions were always preceded by forms of worship: no Athenian assembly could start without sacrificing a piglet, for example, and sprinkling its blood around; no political business was conducted without a statue of Zeus witnessing it.

And yet, vastly different contexts do not automatically undermine the idea that some configurations of spaces have remained remarkably similar because of the functions they serve: political assembly, something recognizable across the centuries, is an example. What's more, the differences we can grasp bring to light some of our hidden, or barely considered, assumptions about what we do when we say we are doing democracy. We are still living with the notion that something called democracy requires a clearly identifiable and highly regulated site of decision-making as well as more open, flexible spaces where largely unpredictable publics come to their own judgements – with the expectation that such judgements eventually feed into formal decision-making.

Yet today we also take it for granted that large spaces should be available for demonstrations – usually against the government or a foreign government. Here a fundamental difference comes into view: the Athenian democracy did not feature anything that we could recognize as a 'state' – a permanent, free-standing public power (never mind a 'deep state').[7] To be sure, there were distinct offices, but most of these were *filled by lot*. The latter expressed the belief in basic political equality, in the sense of everyone's equal, or at least good enough, political capacity: anyone can do the job, except specialized tasks such as commanding a navy; such positions were subject to elections. Of roughly twelve hundred offices, about a hundred were subject to elections; the rest were distributed by lot, with the assumption that the latter reflected the will of the gods. As a result, about a quarter of the citizenry, in any given year, held either a polis office or served on a jury.[8] Lot was also a highly effective anti-corruption device: if you don't know in advance who will occupy an office, you can't know who to bribe. What resulted from this understanding of democracy? Politicians did not campaign in front of crowds; there were no political parties. And citizens did not get together to protest against anything like state action.

As we shall see shortly, republican Rome is a very different story; there the plebs confronted a Senate, with plebeians and the senatorial elite largely fixed in their roles, and with members of both groups occupying offices in a way that would be much more familiar-looking to us.[9] Roman spaces were clearly allocated to different status groups – though, as we'll also see in a moment, simple bodily movements (no, not crowds rushing in!) could shatter such political pre-assignments meant to keep people in their place.

For the ancients, spaces had to be made to enable particular kinds of participation; the shapes came to be associated with different political roles, but what was placed in the spaces also had a pedagogical function. Athenians sought to provide a kind of political confidence booster for their democracy through aesthetic objects: for instance, a prominent stele shows the goddess democracy placing a wreath on a seated man personifying the demos. They also sought to dignify democracy through style: they adorned the Council House, which prepared the agenda for the popular assembly, with Doric columns – while private homes, even the ones of wealthy owners, remained rather modest (and also largely closed to the outside world, unlike the edifices of Roman patricians).[10] Yet iconography and styles were ultimately secondary. Primary were the spaces: the assembly, the theatre, and the citizen juries. Their prominence in the city landscape would have reminded Athenians every day that they were something special compared to their many international rivals: they were democrats.[11] The spaces as such were *media* – a form of pro-democratic propaganda in stone, if you like.

Tightly Packed Together

The agora was initially not meant to provide a specific, iconic image for residents or visitors; the idea of a master plan and an attendant memorable image of the city came later, during Hellenistic and Roman times.[12] Archaeologists have stressed the relative shapelessness of the early *agorai* and the surrounding settlements.[13] This shapelessness could be linked to the notion – again, something fundamentally alien to us – that the polis was not primarily a specific place, but a group of people. The implication? In principle, the city was mobile. The polis, claimed the Athenian general Nicias, was its *men*, not its walls, and in fact no particular place on earth at all.[14] The Athenians could abandon their city entirely, without dissolving themselves as a political entity; they famously did so with their ruse in the Greco-Persian Wars: in 480 BCE they left the physical site known to us as 'Athens' and ended up defeating the seemingly far superior Persian forces at Salamis.[15] Had they truly migrated, however, they would have required another 'empty place'; for there is no democracy without an agora.

Obviously, the cunning fake exile to trick the Persians was an extraordinary moment; the Athenians were not nomads. But the point remains that they conceived of the polis not primarily in territorial terms. Democracy, for the Greeks, was not so much a political system fixed in one place as a capacity to act together among equals (with 'equality' applying only to ethnic Athenian men, to be sure).[16] This collective capacity was generated, not hampered, by the equal right to speak in the assembly; in fact, it required freedom of speech in Athens

5

more broadly, which could also be exercised by women and slaves – something that particularly grated with an anti-democrat like Plato, who complained about Athens as that city which 'loves talk and is full of talk – unlike Sparta or Crete'.[17]

Athenians as a whole were potentially mobile; individual Athenians inside the polis less so. Territorial questions have always mattered for politics; in fact, it's not a stretch to say that Athenian leaders were obsessed with the need to contain tensions between the urban and the rural.[18] City dwellers were in favour of building a navy, expanding trade, and, eventually, creating an empire; those residing in the countryside of Attica (about as large as the duchy of Luxembourg today) felt that Athens's foreign – and, in their eyes, frivolous – entanglements forced them often to leave the land; as enemies like the Spartans kept invading, rural folk were turned into lumpen city dwellers rather than remaining as dignified peasants.[19] Plato and Aristotle came up with an idea of how the cleavage between urban and rural interests might not lead to perpetual conflict: their ideal cities enabled every family to have two houses, one in the city and one in the countryside, close to the border. But no such scheme was ever implemented.[20]

The place where everyone came together informally – and sometimes formally – was the agora. It had not only political functions: there were the popular juries selected by lot; and there were the different markets: as the poet Eubulus observed, in the agora one could buy apples, chickpeas, laws, indictments, waterclocks, and givers of evidence (the Athenians were extremely litigious); it was also the place to obtain news or, for that matter, to accost a prostitute; and, as always, there were sites devoted to religion.[21] Not everyone agreed with such 'mixed use': Aristotle held that, ideally, an agora for commerce should be separated from an agora for politics and law (which would also feature large common meals for free men in order to foster social cohesion).[22]

The early, classical agora was hardly beautified: it was not paved, it was filled with rubbish that Athenians simply dropped there; and, before the installation of latrines, one could see (and smell) plenty of excrement.[23] Yet that did not diminish the agora's enormous symbolic and practical significance: those convicted of a crime were not permitted to enter it, which meant they were cut off from economic and civic life. Eventually, the space was also purposefully dignified, featuring monuments related to democracy: one was the statue group of the Eponymous Heroes, with one hero for each of the ten tribes (it was also here that decrees were put up for all to read or be read to them); the other was the pair of Harmodios and Aristogeiton, the two 'Tyrannicides'. The pair were venerated for having brought the tyranny of the Peisistratids to an end. They were said to have killed the tyrant Hipparchos during the Panathenaic Games in 514 BC. Both assassins paid with their life.[24]

The assembly alone decided about the erection of monuments, and it is an indication of the extraordinary significance the Tyrannicides held in the Athenian political imagination that they were the first two to receive that honour – and no one else did for about a hundred years.[25] Harmodios and Aristogeiton were exemplars: one a beautiful young man, not yet sporting a beard, the other a mature individual who must have participated in many fights. The statues were put in parallel to each other, with both figures forcefully stepping forward as they attack the tyrant with swords. Except that, according to most sources, they did not actually kill the tyrant, but his brother Hippias instead, and the reason for the attack was that Harmodios, Aristogeiton's lover, had been, as one might say today, sexually harassed by Hippias. (The tyranny in fact continued; it was brought down by invading Spartans.)

We cannot know for sure, but the seemingly private motive did not undermine the image of the Tyrannicides: on the contrary, they were exemplars for whom private and public interests coincided.[26] The erection of the statues might also have had further meaning for Athenian status politics (in fact, the politics of statues is always also status politics): aristocrats distrusted ordinary citizens, whom they suspected of always wanting to cut elites down to size. By putting up the statues, the democracy proved that it was prepared to honour extraordinary individuals and their deeds; elites, as long as they made civic efforts, were recognized as such.[27]

While putting elites at ease, the statues of Harmodios and Aristogeiton also promoted a distinct set of democratic ideals: the two citizens are acting in concert – literally in parallel, performing the same gesture – with each exemplifying disciplined action and the notion of an equal share in an important collective endeavour.[28] In his comedy *Lysistrata*, Aristophanes has a veteran enter the agora and imitate the gesture of Aristogeiton: the old man – a survivor of the legendary battle of Marathon – places himself exactly parallel to the statue; he is hallucinating that the Athenian women want to establish a tyranny (when they are merely occupying the Acropolis and denying sex to their menfolk in order to have them settle for a peace agreement between city states during the Peloponnesian War). In another of Aristophanes' plays, *Assemblywomen*, females have assumed power in Athens and are placing the machines for choosing individuals by lot next to the statue of Harmodios – a prime symbol of democracy with its belief in political equality. Monumentality is a means to shape mentalities: it wasn't just meant to beautify political space; it was also to foster a particular set of political attitudes among the people.

Did the agora as such serve specifically as a reminder about democratic equality? Not in any simple sense: citizens could liberally show off differences in wealth and status. At the same time, they could not always be distinguished from metics, the foreign non-citizens engaged in activities from trade to philosophy – what might today be called permanent residents with special skill sets. Citizens could even be confused with slaves. The latter were not automatically servile; another canonical anti-democrat, the mysterious figure known as 'the Old Oligarch', complained that slaves dared to behave rudely and shoved others in the agora. One did not necessarily push back, because one could not be sure whether they were citizens or not.

The agora, then, provided a space where all kinds of people rubbed shoulders and would assume that they could look each other in the eye as being more or less equal. Having multiple uses of the agora, and many people doing different things, might have reinforced a sense that difference did not mean inequality. The latter was seen as a prime threat to the democracy, and the agora featured an infamous mechanism for dealing with it: ostracism. During ostracisms, the agora was cordoned off; citizens then decided whether a particular individual – whose name was to be written on a shard, an *ostrakon* – posed such a threat to the polity that he had to leave the city. Even today, ostracism is deployed to illustrate the dangers of mob rule: demagogues riling up the people to go after unpopular minorities. Except: in ancient Greece there were no speeches; and being ostracized did not mean automatically being judged a politically bad character. Often, someone was made to leave not because of any wrongdoing; rather, the problem was their possessing too much power. Imagine Silvio Berlusconi being banned from running for office, since having such economic might, and control over so many media channels, and potentially becoming a popular prime minister, was just too much for one polity determined to preserve its freedom.

Like many other large, open spaces, the agora served as a site for rituals. The paradox of rituals is that they are always the same – repetition is the point – but they transform their participants. Ostracism, rather than inciting hatred against individuals, provided a focal point for citizens to deepen and demonstrate commitment to the polity – and to make that commitment visible to everyone else present.[29]

The assembly of citizens tasked with legislating did not meet in the agora, but on a hillside west of the Acropolis, about a ten-minute walk south, still known today as the *Pnyx* – a term derived from the Greek word for 'tightly packed together'.[30] It featured different configurations over time, some of the reasons for which we can only guess: at one point the Athenians used the hill itself for seating, which made people look down at the agora as the background to the speaker; then a kind of theatre with raked seating was created opposite the hill, which made it easier to monitor access – important for those intending to control the assembly, but also crucial after citizens started to get paid for attending. At another point, the members of the assembly faced the Acropolis – perhaps yet another reminder of the inevitable religious dimension of politics; at another they primarily looked in the direction of the sea, maybe also a cue about democracy: after all, it was the men in the navy who had always been the greatest supporters of democracy (and Piraeus, the harbour, was always a democratic stronghold). Size varied, too; the space was systematically enlarged, from a capacity for about 6,000 citizens – the quorum for assembly meetings – to perhaps as many as 13,000. Eventually, the assembly moved to the Theatre of Dionysus, which featured a half-circle of ascending rows of seats, just south of the Acropolis.

One of the configurations in which people were tightly packed together also ensured that the speaker had to face the sun – allowing everyone, in theory, clearly to discern his facial expressions; meanwhile, those listening could not only see the speaker but also each other.[31] While seating was not organized by tribe – and, the point bears repeating, nothing like political parties existed – this mutual visibility, what historians have called 'inter-visibility',[32] should be understood as facilitating the formation of political judgements: after all, one might look to others one knew to have particular insight (or interests), for reactions and cues as to how one would want to vote when considering a particular decree.[33] When the outcome of an assembly is uncertain, the expressions of others matter.

Both agora and *Pnyx* were rambunctious, often theatrical places – the very thing Plato criticized when he portrayed democracy as a 'theatrocracy'. Plato also complained about the 'flow' of gossip that went through the streets of Athens, that despised place of free and endless 'talk', where the stones, in his words, echoed the irrational views of the masses (making the city itself the original echo chamber).[34] But gossip, or – put more neutrally – an exchange of views about people as well as public affairs, crucially complemented the work of the official institutions; to the extent that the ancient Greeks had a concept of gossip, it was associated with men – which is to say, *citizens* – and not with women.[35] In particular, citizens were to form judgements in the half-public, half-private spaces provided by the stoas – porticoes or roofed colonnades – bordering the agora.[36]

Sitting or Standing

What might seem self-evident to us – one should have a chance to *sit* through a long, hot day of speeches in an assembly – was a contested issue in the ancient world. The Romans, while imitating many forms of Greek art and architecture, for the longest time resisted building theatres. A theatre they erected in 154 BCE had to be torn down again; when Pompey eventually created a spectacular edifice for 11,000 spectators – with astounding mechanical contraptions to make people and animals appear from underground – he had to justify it as a religious offering of sorts.[37] Other Roman theatres were temporary, with the Senate deciding each year whether wooden structures would be erected or not. Roman stages would be higher and generally taller than in Greek theatres, while *cavea* (seating sections) and stage were integrated – facilitating crowd control. There were no spectacular vistas of sea or landscape as in Athens; instead of a view to the outside, audiences would be facing monumental orders of columns and lavish statues.[38]

On the occasions when Romans voted, they had to wait while standing in long single lines on jetties. That arrangement – with no secret ballot – made it possible to approach (and bribe) individuals from the side, but virtually impossible for citizens to speak to a larger group and co-ordinate action in making their choice; anything like election speeches were also prohibited on the day.[39] Roman elites were constantly worried that if people sat down, they would start talking, form factions, and, in general, cause political trouble.[40] The Athenians literally had all day to vote, though decisions had to be made by sundown; the Romans, forced to stand and often literally kept in line, probably wanted speedier conclusions to any political process. It is more difficult to form political judgements in the absence of inter-visibility.

The Nazi legal theorist Carl Schmitt, taking his cue from Cicero, noted in his diary in 1956: 'The Greek people's assembly sat, the Roman stood! The difference between democracy and republic!'[41] There is something to this contrast. The Athenian democracy only ever included males with the proper ethnic lineage, so it was highly restrictive by today's standards. But within that category, it aspired to an ideal of political equality, expressed most clearly in equal rights to speak, and equal rights to be chosen by lot for offices (including, amazingly, what might roughly be described as the equivalent of the head of state).

Rome, by contrast, stuck to an official division between a senatorial elite on the one side and plebs on the other. To be sure, the latter had their tribunes, and the Romans, like the Greeks, aspired to exercising collective capacity. But such capacity always came down to 'the Senate acting with the People': *Senatus Populusque Romanus*, as the famous formula had it; there was no suggestion that an internally undifferentiated demos simply constituted the polity itself or should think of itself as a collective body with a special ability to act in concert. Status differences were always and everywhere visible – they were signalled in something as basic as clothing (different togas and shoes for different ranks), and they were reflected in the spaces to which different groups were assigned: think, for instance, of atria; what for us might have positive associations as a light-filled space inside an edifice constituted the waiting room for the clients of powerful patricians (who, unlike the Greeks during democratic times, had fairly open houses ostentatiously adorned).

While the Roman Senate was officially only a body giving advice, its offers of advice could not really be refused. The people were nominally in charge, but they never really assembled to sit down in one space, as was the case with the *Pnyx* and the Theatre of Dionysus. Senators tried to reach consensus among themselves and then presented proposals to assembled citizens – what were known as *contiones*. The citizens stood; a magistrate sat above them and literally talked down to the people. That's not to say that such gatherings did not matter. But their function was more like public opinion surveys; if it became clear that a policy might prove truly unpopular, it was simply withdrawn. The result: virtually every law ever officially proposed was approved by the people.[42]

The Romans, then, constantly got people together – but were afraid of assembly (like the Greeks, they were also afraid of the gods, and nothing could happen without their blessing: every political act had to be preceded by checking the auspices, for which special *templa* were built).[43] As a result, gatherings were highly ritualized, and people were arranged in particular configurations, so as to make spontaneous exchange and unpredictable crowd behaviour less likely. And, unlike in Greece, assemblies could not be convoked by the people – meaning the lower classes – themselves. Finally, the Greeks who had the privilege to act in politics all counted – one person, one vote; in Rome, groups made choices, and, given the different ranks among groups, smaller ones could wield much more power than larger ones (so much so that an issue could be decided before everyone had had a chance to cast a vote). The Greeks moved freely, their location did not reveal rank; Roman groups were assigned to areas corresponding to status.

The Roman Forum has often been treated as an equivalent of the Greek agora, yet the word has a much wider presence in our world than 'agora'. The Forum initially indicated something like a fenced-off area and hosted mainly business transactions; only later did it feature the *curia* – where the Roman Senate met – and the *comitium*, the popular assembly.[44] Like the agora, the Forum served as a place for religious rituals. But, much more than the Greek square, it became a place for individual self-promotion, mostly through leaders erecting monuments and, sometimes, creating entirely new fora to commemorate military triumphs.

Caesar erected a statue of himself close to Venus Genetrix, suggesting that he was a descendant of the gods.[45] Caesar also moved the rostra, the stage for the speaker, from the north to the east side of the Forum; beforehand, people could gather around the platform; now they looked at a kind of distant theatre with the Temple of Concord and the Capitoline Hill as background.[46] The more crowded a forum became with monuments, the less it served as a site for political participation.

And, ironically, the less the people mattered, the more they were eventually allowed to assemble in spaces that resembled the Greek ones. Roman elites were eager to keep up constant communication with citizens (and, to be sure, were expected by the people to observe traditional norms of republican behaviour); but, after the end of the Republic, theatres and the circus, rather than *contiones*, became the prime sites of such communication. There people could look at each other properly – but the judgements on which they converged were not political; they were judgements about whether a defeated gladiator should die or not.[47]

Yet Rome also provides an object lesson in how individual conduct can on occasion subvert strategies of assigning different spaces to different groups, even if the separations are literally set in stone. We might shape our buildings, and then they shape us – but we can sometimes also reshape their meanings. Plutarch offers a wonderfully illuminating account of one particular tribune:

> [C. Gracchus] is said to have shown remarkable earnestness in many ways, and especially in this, that whereas all popular orators before him had turned their faces towards the senate and that part of the forum called the 'comitium', he now set a new example by turning towards the other part of the forum as he harangued the people, and continued to do this from that time on, thus

by a slight deviation and change of attitude stirring up a great question, and to a certain extent changing the constitution from an aristocratic to a democratic form; for his implication was that speakers ought to address themselves to the people, and not to the senate.[48]

The built environment suggested a certain dramaturgy of how politics was to be conducted. But the actors could also change the script by relating to particular spaces differently, even changing what today we would call the constitution – with just a slight turn of the body.

We still consider large squares important for democracy, but mostly because we think of them as sites for demonstrations against state power. The very fact that we do so shows that we are accepting a peculiar *representative* understanding of democracy – we take a gap between us and our representatives as given. It also shows that we consider a state standing apart from us as a normal, in fact unavoidable, fact of life; professional politicians come to us to sound us out; we are part of *contiones*, be it in physical or virtual space, much more than being tightly packed together decision-makers in a theatre or on a hill. If anything, we are Romans, with occasional longings, and fleeting actual moments, of being like Athenians.

Why Does It Matter?

The forum as an urban form – less so the agora – has been continuously revived and adapted. Buildings such as the Palazzo della Ragione in Padua were based on the idea of

17

integrating political and judicial functions on the one hand and commercial activity on the other. (On the ground floor, the palace today still hosts markets inside and outside; the empty hall upstairs overwhelms any visitor with its powerful political and legal symbols painted on the ceiling and walls of the enormous assembly room.)

Architects kept designing with the ancient world as a prop of sorts; they could also explain in ever more detail why they did so: printing made it possible to combine the built environment as a medium with books that promoted architectural choices; these often explicitly invoked political principles.[49] Not everyone thought this was a salutary development: the twentieth-century critic Lewis Mumford complained that 'the real misdemeanor of the printing-press was not that it took literary values away from architecture, but that it caused architecture to derive its value from literature'.[50]

Authors advocating representative democracy in the eighteenth century – almost all of the American revolutionaries, many of the French ones – conjured up a caricature of Athenian mobocracy; the latter served as a foil to responsible, not necessarily responsive, representation of the people through distinguished gentlemen, or what Thomas Jefferson touted as a 'natural aristocracy'. The latter envisaged gentlemen locally selecting the supposedly most talented among themselves; those in turn would choose representatives at state level, and so on (the Electoral College, with whole states voting one way, is a distinctly Roman idea). It is in this context that James Madison made his unflattering observations about mobs – shorthand for the dangers of direct democracy. As we saw, the agora and the *Pnyx* enabled mass action, but they were not unstructured in the way the derogatory term 'mob' suggests.

What's more, over time theorists of modern representative government came to understand that the arch-democratic dynamic of agora and *Pnyx* might still apply under very different historical circumstances: the nineteenth-century British liberal John Stuart Mill argued that the functions of agora and forum were now being fulfilled by a free press, a vital instrument for the formation of public opinion (which, however, could also be curated by responsible journalists). As Mill described ancient politics, 'there could be nothing like a regulated popular government, beyond the bounds of a single city-community; because there did not exist the physical conditions for the formation and propagation of a public opinion, except among those who should be brought together to discuss public matters in the same agora'. He went on to explain that 'this obstacle is generally thought to have ceased by the adoption of the representative system. But to surmount it completely, required the press, and even the newspaper press, the real equivalent, though not in all respects an adequate one, of the Pnyx and the Forum'.

With a free press, free physical spaces did not cease to matter. And they still matter today, as we appear to face seemingly infinite online spaces. Every democracy needs both a *Pnyx* with its official assembly and an agora – a place for formal decision-making and one for informal consolidation of political opinions. What happens in the agora, on squares and streets, is obviously not directly binding; as the jurist Christoph Möllers observed, it has no democratic *form*. Yet it does have a democratic *meaning*.[51]

That notion has always been contested by conservatives driven by a fear of uncontrolled and uncontrollable masses. The nineteenth-century British liberal and poet Matthew Arnold, for instance, was deeply opposed to the common man's 'right to march where he likes, meet where he likes, enter where he likes, hoot as he likes, threaten as he likes, smash as he likes'.[52] As soon as large unregulated space opens up, the spectre of the mob appears.[53]

I will turn to an analysis of our present-day *Pnyx*, which is to say the legislature, and of the streets in subsequent chapters. For now, I want us to focus on a space that, in principle, can work for both authoritarian regimes and democracies: the square. Contrary to the long line of thinkers anxious about mobocracy, what happens there does not turn on a distinction between representative and direct democracy, between responsible politics on the one hand and politics responsive to supposedly irrational mass sentiment on the other. Most of what people do and say on squares and streets makes a claim to representativeness; those on squares just happen not to be appointed to any representative office through formal procedures. They are *self-appointed* representatives (which of course does not mean that there will necessarily be an uptake of their claim to represent something or someone).

Before we say more about what all that means specifically in a democracy, it is important to remind ourselves how assembly in physical space matters in the first place – and why, if one goes back to Mill's idea, it could in some respects not be substituted with a free press, nor, for that matter, a more or less free internet. The notion that it might in fact be entirely replaced and that what happens on squares holds no real political meaning any more has been advanced many times since Mill: in 1967, Marshall McLuhan and Quentin Fiore enthused that 'the public, in the sense of a great consensus of separate and distinct viewpoints, is finished . . . the living room has become a voting booth. Participation via television in Freedom Marches, in war, revolution, pollution, and other events is changing *everything*'.[54] Four decades or so later, Democratic Congressman Barney Frank commented, apropos Occupy Wall Street, that he did not understand 'why people think that simply being in a physical place does much'.[55] Evidently, many people have thought that it does do something: the 2010s, according to one estimate, witnessed more mass protests than any previous era in human history;[56] in particular, the decade saw prominent occupations of public squares, resulting in novel expressions such as 'movements of the squares' or even 'peoples of the square'.

More recent years, by contrast, appear overshadowed by assembly as threat: plenty of governments – including more or less well-functioning democracies – have passed legislation that renders people coming together in particular places more difficult. Just think of the UK Public Order Act of 2023, with its vague, in many ways arbitrary, notion of 'public disruption'; or note the tendency in the United States to displace protestors onto designated 'zones' and 'bubbles' – a faint echo of the Roman practice of placing potentially troublesome plebs in assigned spaces.[57]

A right to assemble is officially acknowledged in all democracies, usually with the qualification of 'peaceful' – something not deemed necessary when guaranteeing the right to free speech and the right freely to associate. But how exactly assembly matters for democracy is far from self-evident. Does taking a stance necessarily mean taking a particular place?[58] Will any square do; in fact, are squares as such 'equitable and democratic', because they provide 'common ground', in the words of the writer Catie Marron?[59] Are squares per se connected to dissent, as suggested in the Italian phrase *scendere in piazza* – to go to protest (though, in other languages, the idiom refers to going *on*, or descending *into*, *the street*)? Can we really point to factors that allow us to judge one square 'more democratic' than another?

First, we must get clear on why assembly matters at all, especially when it has become so much easier to connect to others without assembling in the same physical space (or, for that matter, getting news without having to amble to the agora, or even just the local newsagent). Evidently, assembly is not democratic as such. People can be assembled simply to acclaim a dictator – the use of large squares in Nicolae Ceaușescu's Romania (1960s–1980s) or in today's China are examples, and of course those in Nazi Germany.[60]

Clearly, people have to be able to assemble freely, in a *double sense*: they should be able to come together voluntarily, and they must retain freedom in how they conduct themselves when they stand or sit together. Both conditions are not met in the stereotypical mass acclamations in dictatorships, when individuals are *forced* together – not voluntarily packed together, as on the *Pnyx* – and made into a compact collective, with all spaces in between, for free speech and action, destroyed or shut down.[61]

So, what happens when individuals come together freely? First, there is assembly as message or, if you prefer, *making something manifest* – an idea that comes out clearly in the French word *manifestation*.[62] One thing one can generally read from assembly most easily is numbers. Here, people coming together is understood primarily as a form of proclamation, not argumentation;[63] the more people assemble, the more clearly a gathering indicates that an issue matters. Leaders in the civil-rights movement kept invoking 'the meaning of our numbers'; Trump and his acolytes confirmed the point apropos the disputes about attendance at his January 2017 presidential inauguration.[64]

The sociologist Charles Tilly summed up the issues with a memorable, if not necessarily elegant, abbreviation: assemblies can manifest 'WUNC': worthiness, unity, numbers, and commitment.[65] Many citizens are willing to shoulder costs, inconveniences, perhaps even hardships to get to a particular place – simple as that. Walt Whitman wrote: 'I and mine do not convince by arguments: we convince by our presence'.[66]

In some situations, numbers matter especially because those assembling wish distinctly to show that they are *more* than a particular other group. In demonstrations against contemporary far-right populist parties, the point has been, among other things, to dispute their self-presentation as speaking for 'the silent majority'. In one instance the slogan of the counter-mobilization said simply 'we are more' or 'there are more of us' – a statement that, needless to say, does not delegitimate the right of a loud minority to make itself heard.[67]

People perceiving sheer numbers might distinctly embolden them. Of course, global views were hardly available before the invention of photography and television (and the use of helicopters to film crowds from above, something first done by the press for the 1960s riots in Los Angeles and by the police for the 1968 protests in Paris).[68] A socialist newspaper once suggested that May Day parades in Vienna should feature a platform on the side of the marchers, so that every participant could momentarily step up and see how huge the numbers were.[69] The observation that certain spaces enable recognition, even self-affirmation, is not new: Goethe remarked on how, in the arena of Verona, *das Volk*, quite apart from the spectacle it could observe, was put in an excellent position to admire *itself*.[70]

Being there is one thing, truly doing something together is another. Assemblies can inspire a sense of collective capacity; here is a plausible analogy with the Athenians. In his advice to the Poles on how to design a constitution for a freedom-loving people, Rousseau recommended that they institute festivities and 'many public games where the good mother country delights in seeing her children at play' – in contrast with 'shut-in halls' and 'dissolute effeminate theatres' in which people would just passively consume entertainment.[71]

The *fêtes* of the French Revolution sought to make this aspiration a reality. They featured a dramaturgy of citizens moving through different parts of Paris, often so as to revisit, or even re-enact, crucial moments of the Revolution. The very first revolutionaries simply repurposed existing rituals: those who had stormed the Bastille afterwards proceeded to the Hôtel de Ville, parading on pikes the heads of the commandant of the Bastille, the Marquis de Launay, as well as a municipal official suspected of treason. They were in fact using royal rituals – the procession and the display of maximally cruel punishment – to claim legitimacy for what they had done: the murders had not been a crime; rather, they had constituted an exercise in new-found popular sovereignty.[72]

Using carefully selected Parisian spaces was crucial for getting that claim to legitimacy across.

With the later *fêtes*, citizens were specifically meant to observe each other being engaged in affirming the right political ideals – but not necessarily forming their own views on what these ideals meant exactly. What was supposed to be made manifest was unity; hence no space for discussion during which people might develop different notions of what the whole thing was about. Rousseau had conceived of festivals as ideally a kind of male brotherhood, resembling a homogeneous military regiment (another problem he had with theatres was that men and women freely mixed).[73] Like the assembly in his model polity – described in his most famous political essay, *The Social Contract* – people were supposed to look at each other and look inward, concentrating intently on the common good; like the Romans, they weren't really supposed to talk with each other. It was mute inter-visibility, with, ideally, no variations in expressions of republican enthusiasm.

Political festivals in revolutionary France, then, were not out-of-control carnivals; if anything, they kept being modelled on Catholic and royal processions. And here as well, rituals – repeating what had come before, even if the political content had been radically different – were meant to be both performative and *transformative*: ordinary men would be turned into proud, patriotic republican citizens. Celebrations, by contrast, might also draw on rituals, but they could be much more creative – and they might not transform people at all.[74] In fact, they might more plausibly reveal people for what they have been all along, as they get drunk. Rituals usually make people put on a mask; festivals can make them drop their masks.

Rousseau was extremely rigid in his prescriptions for assembly; others see the value of assembly precisely in creating largely uncontrollable moments of collective effervescence and occasions for *jouissance*. The Marxist historian Eric Hobsbawm observed that, 'next to sex, the activity combining bodily experience and intense emotion to the highest degree is the participation in a mass demonstration at a time of great public exaltation'. He went on to explain that 'unlike sex, which is essentially individual, it is by its nature collective. Like sex it implies some physical action – marching, chanting slogans, singing – through which the merger of the individual in the mass, which is the essence of the collective experience, finds expression'.[75]

In such moments we might overcome what Elias Canetti, the great twentieth-century novelist and psychologist of crowds, saw as a primal fear. Canetti wrote that 'there is nothing that man fears more than the touch of the unknown'. Hobsbawm's 'merger of the individual in the mass' constitutes a rare exception; because we know that we are in this together – because we want to be in this together – that fear disappears.

Marching or Settling Down

There is more at stake in assembly than those assembled recognizing unity and commitment *to each other*: manifestations wish to communicate something, including unity and numbers, to a wider audience. Unlike with Rousseau's festival, an audience beyond the immediate participants is necessary if the intention is to get across a particular message, as well as an indication of numbers, unity, and commitment. The philosopher Slavoj Žižek dismissed aspects of Occupy Wall Street by saying that carnivals come cheap.[76] But carnivals are usually not just for the people in masks.

If the point is to reach an audience, assemblies should happen where others are already present, even if for completely apolitical reasons. The American urban theorist William 'Holly' Whyte, who single-handedly created a scientific field of studying plazas and street corners in big cities, put it best: 'what attracts people most, it would appear, is other people'. (He added: 'It is difficult to design a space that will not attract people. What is remarkable is how often this has been accomplished.')[77] Being able to assemble and manifest in front of others allows one to be in their face, so to speak, and, ideally, to draw them into some kind of engagement. One can block others on the web; as a civilian, one can usually not remove someone insisting on getting a political message across in a public place.

Beyond WUNC, assemblies can serve the purpose of meeting, understood now as distinctly argumentative, not proclamative: those assembling do not simply affirm unity and commitment, they engage with each other over longer periods, be it about programmes or questions of tactics and strategy. And some people might simply be there to learn something. The US Supreme Court at one point affirmed, apropos public forums, that '[e]ven in the modern era, these places are still essential venues for public gatherings to celebrate some views, to protest others, or simply to learn and inquire' – a seemingly anodyne observation, but one of the few that picks up on the possibility of learning in public, or, for that matter, learning through the public.[78]

27

Meetings to 'learn and inquire' might be more likely to take place indoors, and the right to gather indoors generally enjoys far higher levels of legal protection; it is virtually never subject to prior restraint. Some cases are in between: Nuit debout, the 2016 social movement opposing changes in French labour law that made a point of its participants staying up all night on Paris's Place de la République, as well as Occupy in NYC, were less about forming stable associations; they were about finding outdoor spaces for continuous discussions. These movements claimed space for encampment; within that space, they tried to set up smaller and separate meeting places where specialized inquiries could take place. What might have looked to casual observers like a chaotic tent city was in fact carefully structured.

Beyond WUNC and meetings, there is performance, in the traditional sense of 'putting on a show'. Theatrical elements of assemblies can serve different purposes: they might contribute to unity and commitment if they symbolically condense a message around which participants can rally; they might be interactive, going beyond speeches, such that performance shades into meeting.

For both meetings and performances, a distinction coined by Elias Canetti is helpful: he divided crowds into open and closed ones.[79] Open ones, by definition, could be joined by more and more people; closed ones, by contrast, somehow managed to control access. An example illustrates what is at stake: Tahrir Square in Cairo, with its many large entrances, remained an open space throughout the Egyptian Revolution in early 2011.[80] The vast square – bordering the Egyptian Museum, a mosque, an enormous administrative building (the distinctly Soviet-looking Mogamma), and the headquarters of the Arab League – was a kind of leftover space from a late nineteenth-century urban plan to transform the Egyptian capital into a Paris of the Middle East, with wide boulevards. It had served as a site of protest before, but in every single case the regime had cracked down hard immediately. That is why occupying and then holding the Square became an achievement in its own right.

In January and February 2011 those assembled included secular citizens, Christians, and members of the Muslim Brotherhood; Tahrir Square acquired its own institutions to organize collective life, but it also stayed accessible to basically anyone who wanted to join. Under the slogan 'Freedom, Bread, and Social Justice', Christians formed a protective circle around praying Muslims; a Christian girl poured water for Muslim ablutions; Muslims and Christians sometimes joined in prayer; Salafis sat peacefully with citizens who appeared entirely secular.[81]

The situation was different in Rabaa Square – not really

Tahrir Square: The Mogamma is in the background.

a square at all, but a large intersection on the main road to the Cairo airport. There access was regulated by members of the Muslim Brotherhood, who were protesting the military's removal of President Muhammad Morsi from office. The space also became a large camping ground, but room for expression was much more limited; effectively, only Muslim prayers were allowed.[82] Entrance to the encampment was tightly controlled.

Our task here is not to pass judgement on the politics of the two assemblies; rather, it is to underline that open versus closed has significant implications for the functions of argument, meeting, and even performance: strengthening internal cohesion is just a different goal than reaching, and possibly convincing, uncommitted audiences who can drop in and out at will.

The distinction matters for yet another function of assembly: what social scientists call 'prefigurative politics'. For not all demonstrations are reducible to 'demands' and

Rabaa Square: Doesn't seem like much of a square. The mosque that must not be photographed is outside the frame on the left.

'grievances' addressed to existing authorities (whose legitimacy protestors, by definition, ultimately accept – otherwise why address the authorities?).[83] Lasting assemblies have frequently erected structures that served not only internal debate but were meant to demonstrate to others how human beings might relate to each other in ways not yet practised in a society.

There are two scenarios: an already unified movement displays unfamiliar practices that 'prefigure' and thereby inspire others; or, second scenario, a much more heterogeneous set of different groups tries to come together, maybe just barely united around goals but committed to being in a particular space, and only gradually working out new forms of living together. This was one meaning of what the people in Tahrir Square were doing; a few years later, in the winter of 2013–14, the Maidan in Kyiv turned into a 'laboratory of the social contract'.[84]

As citizens are thrown together in shared space – overcoming Canetti's fear of touch – a relatively easy sociability can develop: barriers to interaction are removed by the common experience of hardship, or the sense of a threat faced together, or just the sheer intensity generated by a collective purpose (though it can also mean, as participants of Occupy Wall Street reported, that their stuff was stolen when they didn't look).[85] Basic needs of food, shelter, and security have to be taken care of; sometimes there is even something like a lost-and-found office (in Tahrir Square, one older man with a large bag who became known to everyone).[86]

Holding the square – endurance – is a straightforward way of communicating commitment; and it can take extreme forms: Brian Haw, protesting against British policies vis-à-vis

Iraq with posters, camped opposite the British Parliament for close to ten years, beginning in 2001. During that time he lost his job, and he lost his family; he also witnessed how the people across the road several times tried to pass legislation that would have allowed his removal by police. In 2011, three months before that legislation finally was to come into effect, Haw, a chain-smoker, died of lung cancer in Berlin, where he had been receiving treatment. In 2007 the artist Mark Wallinger won the Turner Prize on account of his exhibition 'State Britain' at the Tate Gallery; Wallinger had painstakingly re-created 600 items confiscated by police from Haw's camp, be it the tarpaulin shelter or the tea-maker.[87] Haw himself visited the museum often; Wallinger observed after Haw's death: 'His rectitude was a mirror that the people in the building opposite couldn't bear.'[88]

As an occupation lasts, people can offer entertainment and education: the Maidan featured a piano (painted in the Ukrainian national colours), so did Taksim Square in Istanbul at the time of the Gezi Park protests; 'free universities' get established, reminiscent of the idea of a 'parallel polis' that Central European dissidents were creating alongside authoritarian state socialist institutions in the 1970s and 1980s.[89] Such parallel poleis prefigure by acting as if a particular future was already present. Those publicly exercising the rights that a regime promises but in practice denies or those appearing in public and putting forward a claim to political standing – think of suffragists who acted as if they were fully emancipated already – thereby show to others, and prove to themselves, what is possible.

Spaces of prefigurative politics can also be more or less open. In principle, an assembly with clearly visible structures, such as temporary buildings, can be accessible to anyone passing by;[90] the division between those consciously assembled and onlookers is much less obvious and strict than is the case with marches. For marches create boundaries – you either move in one direction or you don't; encampments can remain porous.[91] The latter therefore also create a certain ambivalence. Being inside them does not mean you have joined a cause; you might just be checking it out; marching appears to be a much clearer commitment.[92]

Prefigurative politics differs fundamentally, then, from what one might call – and this is not meant to be dismissive – *petition politics*. The latter addresses the powers-that-be; those engaged in it *demonstrate for or against something*. Those doing prefigurative politics, by contrast, *demonstrate something*. The two are not always mutually exclusive; successful prefiguration can be a step towards petition: in the first half of the nineteenth century a figure like the socialist entrepreneur Robert Owen was proving that a more humane form of organizing work was possible through his own factory communities in Lancashire; but he also lobbied politicians in London and Washington, DC – where he spoke in the House of Representatives – to change policies on child labour and the length of the workday at the national level.[93]

Differences between petition and prefiguration do not neatly map onto a distinction between moderate and radical. Exercises in civil disobedience can look radical – think of some of the actions by Extinction Rebellion, effectively bringing parts of London to a standstill by blocking bridges or targeting the Underground at rush hour. Yet the whole point of such law-breaking is to appeal to a majority to see the arguments of the protestors and change policies as a result; the political system as such is not necessarily put into question. By contrast, open encampments can look like harmless hippie gatherings – yet their motivation might be to offer practices that could substitute entirely for politics as we know it. For the politics of petition, both squares and streets are helpful; 'the sheer meaning of our numbers' can be showcased in them, but the more traditional forms of addressing the powerful, such as literally writing petitions to parliamentarians, might also do. Prefiguration, by contrast, needs a place, and the square will provide the kind of space that the street cannot.

Assemblies might change what a space means. A square may have been known as a parade ground for an authoritarian regime or as a site for exercising colonial power. Assemblies with certain messages, or sometimes direct action on the built environment, change what a particular space evokes. Think of Grand Parade in Cape Town, with its city hall made from stones imported from Britain and designed to look like a version of precious Bath. It meant something different before and after Nelson Mandela spoke there hours after being released from twenty-seven years in prison.

Contactless Democracy?

Could the functions discussed so far be fulfilled in cyberspace?[94] After all, politicians are telling us that 'social media platforms are increasingly serving as today's town squares',[95] a view echoed, among many others, by the US Supreme Court.[96]

Some answers would seem to be straightforward: sheer

numbers also matter in virtual space. Think of how a hitherto unknown teenager, Emma González, a survivor of the 2018 Parkland school shooting in Florida, could surpass the NRA in numbers of followers on what was known at the time as Twitter.[97] Two problems, though: for one thing, are the numbers real, or might they have been generated by bots? We cannot see an actual mass of people online in the way that individual citizens become visible in physical space (think back to the platform the Viennese socialists installed to give everyone the chance to survey the crowd as a whole).[98] And even if the online denizens are real, are they given particular prominence by algorithms none of us understand?[99]

That algorithms in the widest sense of that term include and exclude is hardly new: so-called traditional media obviously gave power to editors to select what news was fit to print and broadcast. The difference is that with these media there was a better chance of guessing leanings and selection criteria, and also of knowing where to look for alternative sources of information and commentary.

What's new about the internet is not manipulation; it's that it is so often impossible to tell whether one is being manipulated. What is also new is that the messages we receive are highly personalized, while the origins of the message appear largely impersonal. Is the person bringing us the news more like a mailman or an editor; are sites and platforms best understood as mechanisms for delivery, common carriers of information, if you like, or are they news media themselves, with attendant gatekeeping functions?[100] True, if a platform is owned by a far-right activist (who happens to be the planet's wealthiest individual), and that person makes no secret of what is being amplified and what is being banned (and why), there is some clarity as to who and what one is dealing with. But, for the most part, what's behind the screen is invisible; we simply cannot tell. What we can tell at best is that someone wants our attention – but we cannot tell how exactly they decide on the best way to retain it, and how far they might go to retain it (and, in the end, why they seem to be succeeding).

Online, the significance of numbers might only have the most tenuous relationship to levels of commitment. 'Liking' and sharing are nowhere close to the investment that offline demonstrations require – not to speak of the potential risks to physical bodies that are put on the line by being put on streets and squares. Initial difficulties and risks make it more likely for a movement to succeed in the long run. Time-consuming organization-building means that resilient structures will be in place when the state pushes back; at the very least, an organization will be able to 'talk to the state', as it has designated representatives (as opposed to the state – or journalists, for that matter – picking which supposed representatives they like best).[101]

Yet this contrast is a little too simple. Think again about possible risks: offline, it is often possible to disappear into a crowd. In some countries, you can legally wear a mask (in any case, after COVID, laws against masking are not the same any more). Such asymmetrical visibility – you can see and identify them; they can't see and identify you – is reversed online: three dozen trackers might be 'watching' you, not to speak of the state itself.[102] Of course, the same risks apply if you bring your cellphone to the march – but that is a choice, whereas online, with many platforms, there simply is not much of a choice.[103]

The issue of anonymity in politics is complex and has received too little attention. I will return to it later, as we consider claims to privacy in public places like the street; for now, I just want to flag that one cannot take for granted that publicity and democracy always neatly go together. As a US Supreme Court decision affirmed in 1995, doing politics in a public space without revealing one's identity can be justified in the face of overbearing majorities eager to clamp down on unpopular views.[104] Facebook's 'real name' policy has been disadvantageous to dissenters in many authoritarian countries, as has been the reliance on 'communities' enforcing norms, when the communities in question are simply doing the bidding of authoritarians.[105]

Can the internet become a site of collective-capacity building? Obviously, citizens might more easily find each other when they wish to make common cause. Yet it's much harder to see what 'doing things in common' can really mean online beyond converging on a demand, or, more likely, shared outrage. And what would prefigurative politics even mean, given that the very simple things that can signal commitments offline – bring a book to the free public library, cook soup for the people holding the Maidan during the coldest winter hours – would appear to be unavailable online?

The idea that 'filter bubbles' make doing things together easier is mistaken on several levels: for one thing, the common diagnosis of 'filter bubbles' and 'echo chambers' is empirically dubious.[106] And while certain platforms are gigantic machines generating confirmation bias, they are not completely isolating particular 'communities'. They are better understood as machines that maximize mutual irritation:

not so much bubbles as clashes of bubbles.[107] For irritation, indignation, and outrage keep us hooked; and that allows our presence and revelations about ourselves to be monetized – a dynamic simply absent from physical public space.

Now, how we communicate online is not necessarily more radical; and not all mutual irritation is a bad thing. But our communication might also subtly be *gamified*: who gets the largest number of responses, who makes the cleverest memes?[108] Some forms of engagement can seem to reduce distance and strangeness, but without the *potentially* exhilarating sense of physically being touched by strangers and touching strangers – the experience Canetti and Hobsbawm highlighted.[109] Online outrage may feel particularly visceral – but it's also always possible to click away or scroll further down, and avoid having someone be in your face.

Not all aspects of democracy require physical proximity, but an entirely contactless democracy is no democracy at all. That leaves the question whether squares and streets will both do for democratic contact, or if there is something special about squares. One possible advantage of squares: every march will eventually come to an end; an occupation on a square, by contrast, might last a very long time and hence maximize opportunities for what one might hope could be productive forms of mutual irritation.[110] But will any square do?

Finally on the Square

Is there an inherently democratic square, in the way that, for instance, the British architect David Adjaye has suggested?[111]

Not really. But different kinds of spaces can facilitate different functions of assembly: closed squares, as advocated by many late nineteenth-century urban planners, and open, usually car-friendly ones, as advocated by many modernists, offer very different possibilities.[112] As we saw above, assemblies themselves can be open or closed; evidently, open meetings and open forms of prefigurative politics are helped by spaces that are accessible and feel porous. Tahrir, with the many streets leading into it, was impossible to close off; Rabaa, as basically just one major intersection, was relatively easy to control.

For manifestations in the sense described above, it helps for squares to be large, even if such a space does not have to equate with a modernist architectural fantasy of isolated objects in space and continuous voids.[113] They just need to be large enough, central enough, attract enough people, and provide space for both assembly and, depending on what people want to do, enough room for performances or pre-figuration within assembly.

Historically, it was often seen as a sign of creeping autocracy if squares became filled with smaller buildings or monuments, as was the case with the Loggia on the Piazza della Signoria in republican Florence and, as we already saw, the crowding of the Roman Forum with ever more statues under various self-promoting Caesars. To be sure, numbers here are relative: the logic of the Place Royale, pioneered in Paris by Henri IV and Louis XIV, is a square's complete focus on *one* royal statue; it was more, not less, authoritarian than a forum with many statues.[114]

Making a square into a 'living room' or salon, while seemingly attractive at first sight, can also detract from its capacity to host what I have been calling manifestations; it was Napoleon who built a banqueting hall on the west side of St Mark's Square, declaring the piazza 'le plus grand salon d'Europe'.[115] In principle, unprogrammed, not overly declamatory, and what has also been called 'loose space' is helpful for manifestations; or, drawing on a distinction coined by Michael Walzer: space needs to be sufficiently 'open-minded' (as opposed to 'single-minded', like the shopping mall, let alone the aeroplane).[116]

Then again, some large squares are simply too large: they basically serve as parade grounds, or for other ceremonies (as opposed to spontaneous celebrations). People cannot help but feel, or de facto get, lost in them. Tiananmen is an example – it had been enlarged under Mao, who at one point supposedly demanded that it should accommodate a billion people; one finds the same problem with Red Square in Moscow.[117] The issue is not just size, but singular use. As we saw, Aristotle already asked for a clear separation between an agora for politics and an agora for market activity; this vision was eventually realized, tellingly, when Athenian democracy was over, under the Roman Emperor Hadrian. But large squares with purely political purposes are ones where citizens have no ordinary business. 'Mixed use' does not necessarily denigrate politics; rather, it leaves open the possibility that the political might emerge from all kinds of interactions and occasions initially not deemed political at all.

Large squares are evidently good for performances: Tiananmen was advantageous for the theatrics centred on the seven-metre tall Goddess of Democracy, a mixture of Statue of Liberty and traditional Asian statues (eventually, a tank drove into it at full speed, destroying it completely).[118]

But squares are often not suitable for meetings, especially if large assemblies are then supposed to be divided into smaller groups, or forms of prefigurative politics might end up feeling marginal in a very large space. So, arguments about size and unprogrammed space – appropriate for manifestations – are now turned on their head: a space can be, or at least can feel, too large; it provides no structure or simply is, or just feels, too exposed. That's one reason why the design theorist Christopher Alexander wanted to limit the size of squares to seventy feet or so in length (advising, in general: 'Make a public square much smaller than you would at first imagine').[119]

A sense of having too much space was reported by participants in Nuit debout on the Place de la République. Indeed, while the square is hardly unstructured, it seems relatively undifferentiated in comparison with other Parisian squares; what's more, it is surrounded on all sides by heavy traffic flows, without any real intermediate zones featuring grass or trees – which is the case on another square in Paris conventionally associated with left-wing agitation, Place de la Nation.

Some squares appear almost domestic: the Place des Vosges in Paris, originally Place Royale, is one example.[120] A little like the ancient agora – which, after all, covered a relatively small area – such more intimate squares might also provide semi-sheltered spaces like arcades, stoas, spaces in which one can retreat for somewhat more private exchanges or meetings but ones that are supposed to remain accessible for passers-by, unlike ones in interior spaces, which one will hardly come across spontaneously. Seating, especially something that can be moved and put together in creative configurations, is helpful; it increases the time spent in public space by fifteen minutes or so.[121]

Proximity Counts

States create what the urbanist Henri Lefebvre called 'monumental space' as an expression of their power.[122] But such large, often ceremonial, in many ways overwhelming spaces are under exceptional circumstances – in moments of real political upheaval – also available for oppositional assemblies. Examining what he calls 'urban civic episodes' in the twentieth and twenty-first century, the political scientist Mark Beissinger finds that protest in 'monumental public space' relies on the power of numbers (rather than the power of arms); he also notes that 'urban revolutionary episodes that have engaged in rallies, protests, or processions in public space have had a significantly higher rate of success than those which engage in other tactics but do not use demonstrations – irrespective of the level of mass participation involved'.[123]

Beissinger contrasts rural rebellions in the twentieth century, the success of which depended on conquering hearts and minds among villagers, with urban uprisings in the post-Cold War period, where control of urban space has been the crucial variable. As recently as 1968, the social scientist Samuel Huntington could assert that 'he who controls the countryside controls the country'.[124] With large-scale urbanization and, in particular, the rise of urban middle classes ready to protest corruption and develop a new civic repertoire of largely peaceful protest, both rural and urban guerrilla warfare ceased to be a method of bringing about change.

Most significant for our discussion here: Beissinger finds that proximity to the edifices where the authorities reside – usually on large squares – is a particularly important factor for the outcome of these 'episodes'. He notes that 'a majority of successful urban civic revolts occurred within seven hundred meters of the seat of power. By contrast, a majority of failed urban civic episodes occurred at least 2.9 kilometers from the seat of power.'[125]

So, proximity matters; and, when not close to power-holders, a square should at least have symbolic power. The journalist Ari Shavit laments that on Rabin Square in Tel Aviv protestors are merely 'gathering at the foot of the terrace of an unimportant municipal building in a square demarcated by nondescript residential blocks'. He goes on to observe that 'all they are doing is standing on the beige granulite tiles and waiting for the helicopters from the evening news to document them and estimate their number and report that Rabin Square is again overflowing with protesters'. He concludes wistfully that their anguish simply has no real address.[126]

Large spaces close to seats of power provide a focal point for protest; such protest increases the potential for disrupting the business of government (that can also take a more indirect form, though: the Egyptian military found it embarrassing that the camp on Rabaa Square was blocking the route to the airport for everyone, including foreign dignitaries). Yet proximity to power – and visibility in a large space – simultaneously renders protestors more vulnerable to repression, which leads Beissinger to identify a 'repression-disruption tradeoff'.[127]

To be sure, half-way functioning democracies are not the subject of revolts in the same way as were kleptocratic autocracies like those of Egypt's Hosni Mubarak and Ukraine's Viktor Yanukovych. But the basic trade-offs can be similar, in particular in an age when states seem more willing to crack down on particular people (known climate protestors are put into preventive detention); on proclamations (certain expressions whose meaning is debatable are now considered indissolubly associated with Hamas, for instance, and hence are grounds for prohibition of assemblies in Germany), and possessions (in the UK, all kinds of objects might now be considered fit for 'locking on' and can therefore be reason for an arrest even when an individual has taken no action at all that would suggest a desire to 'lock on').[128]

Proximity to power might also make assembly somewhat predictable. In matters of location and symbolism, one of the most interesting aspects of the French Yellow Vests Movement (*Mouvement des gilets jaunes*) was its occupation of traffic roundabouts; it made their cause very visible, articulating, in conjunction with the yellow warning vests, a sense that they were simply not being seen by the Macron government. The location of display directly pointed to a main source of grievances: the price of diesel. But, above all, it was an innovative choice of protest sites, which evidently took the state by surprise; it mattered that those engaged in assembly deviated from a routinized *système manifestant*.[129]

Laying Siege

The German philosopher Jürgen Habermas has extensively theorized what he sees as the necessarily dual character of democracy: formal law-making on the one side, the never-ceasing flows of communication, which eventually crystallize as public opinion, on the other: by now we recognize this as the duality of *Pnyx* and agora. Habermas has also suggested an arresting image for the relationship between public debate and the site of collectively binding decisions by representatives: citizens, he writes, should lay *siege* to the representative institutions. But – this is the paradoxical point of the image – it is a siege that must never succeed; citizens should not conquer the institutions on which they are putting pressure.[130] Only elections can decide who occupies what Louis Kahn called 'legislative palaces'.

Elections make for certainty about who occupies the seats of formal authority. Democracy is best understood as a system characterized by what the political scientist Adam Przeworski has called institutionalized uncertainty.[131] That mouthful refers to a simple thought, one that is also behind the idea that democracy and abstraction, or, if you prefer, disembodiment, are somehow connected – the idea intimated in John Quincy Adams's pronouncements about iconoclasm: in democracies, we do not know who will be authorized by elections (or other mechanisms, like lot) to rule; but we *do* know the procedures for finding office-holders and also for arriving at collectively binding decisions. In short, there's uncertainty about outcomes; but there is certainty about institutions. In autocracies, it is the reverse: people know who will rule, but the procedures – such as election laws – can be changed any time. Just think of Putin fiddling with voting regulations for presidential elections until the last minute to ensure that Alexei Navalny's campaigns had no chance.

To say that there's certainty about institutions in democracies is not to suggest that these are immutable. They can be criticized in the name of the underlying principles justifying democracy – freedom and equality – and be transformed through popular pressure. To highlight institutional certainty is also not to claim that democracy is reducible to procedures. Institutions that enable collectively binding decisions are subject to continuous judgement by citizens; decision-making in the political system and informal public debate form a continuous process. Elections should not be understood as mechanisms for a one-off aggregation of static preferences, but part of an ongoing back-and-forth of arguing about policy – as well as the meaning of fundamental political principles for that matter.[132]

'Arguing' hints at one final assumption: democracy obviously needs some political settlement; not all institutions can be up for grabs all the time. But it's a mistake to equate democracy with consensus or civility. A free society in which citizens confront each other as equals is bound to produce conflict; and public space matters not least because it's where people can get in each other's faces. After all, as the jurist Christopher Essert underlines, public space is unique in one regard: here no private person can tell another how they are allowed to act.[133] That freedom includes a freedom to engage others on one's own terms; the exercise of that liberty can be annoying, sometimes very annoying, but democracy guarantees no such thing as a right not to be annoyed by one's fellow citizens.

So, conflict is perfectly legitimate in a democracy, part of whose value precisely consists in allowing us to deal with conflict in a peaceful manner. Elections settle conflicts – but only temporarily; at least in theory, democracies always allow political decisions to be re-opened; they enable what the political theorist Nadia Urbinati has called a politics of second thoughts.[134]

As we already saw, it matters that the articulation of second thoughts and the instigation of peaceful conflicts is allowed to happen not too far from the actual seats of power. It is an advantage in a democracy if legislatures have large, uncluttered spaces on one side, what in Canberra is known by the somewhat Orwellian name 'Authorized Assembly Space'. These spaces do not have to be purely political nor feel like 'space without qualities'. But they also should not be overly landscaped, or symbolically over-programmed, such that creative collective self-expression becomes difficult.[135]

Legislators have used the programming of their surroundings as an argument to keep citizens safely away. The latter found such reasoning phony, and, in the United States, judges eventually agreed with them: note a US District Court's ruling on whether there could be demonstrations on the Capitol Grounds in Washington, DC. The Court stated that 'the only governmental interests that the Government has cited which would justify excluding all demonstrations are the "peace", "serenity", "majesty", maintenance of a "park-like setting"', and the 'glorification of a form of government through visual enhancement of its public buildings'. It went on to point out that 'ranged against these "interests" is the right to assemble and to petition for the redress of grievances'. The judges delivered the coup de grâce by pointing out that 'the desire of Congress, if such there be, to function in the "serenity" of a "park-like setting" is fundamentally at odds with the principles of the First Amendment', whose 'function . . . under our system of government is to invite dispute', and which 'may indeed best serve its high purpose when it induces a condition of unrest, creates dissatisfaction with conditions as they are, or even stirs people to anger'.[136] This decision ended the decades-long period when marchers on Washington never turned up in front of Congress (considered by many protestors a more important branch of government than the Presidency); there had been a reason why the most famous march in American history, Martin Luther King's 'March on Washington for Jobs and Freedom', was directed to the Lincoln Memorial, rather than confronting the legislature.

Now, particular assembled people are not the same as 'the people' themselves; in fact, 'the people' can never fully appear in a democracy, nor can they be fully represented without someone possibly objecting that they in fact do not feel represented. What parts of the people (never '*the* people') can do, though, is indeed march on Washington, so to speak. To make sections of the people visible – especially those who feel excluded or forgotten – is obviously part of the democratic function of public space. By contrast, to shout on the square 'We are the people' in a half-way functioning democracy has neither democratic form – to pick up the distinction developed by Möllers again – nor democratic meaning.[137] It is what authoritarian populists do as they claim that they, and only they, represent what they often call 'the silent majority' or also 'the real people' – the very address Donald Trump used for his supporters on the Ellipse (the President's Park South) on 6 January 2021, just before the assault on the Capitol. That claim comes with an attempt symbolically to prescribe how 'the real people' are to be understood once and for all, closing off future contestation and any possible second thoughts on questions of membership of the people.

Obviously other politicians, and activists for that matter, can also make claims about the character of the people – people-talk is not automatically populist, and it would be absurd to declare it out of bounds in a democracy. But populists offer such talk not as a fallible and falsifiable proposition, but as a claim beyond contestation.

The German political scientist Philip Manow has suggested that the reflection of representative buildings in a pool – the 'reflecting pool' – might symbolize the fluid, impermanent nature of democratic representation: neither the assembly nor assembled citizens ever fully represent the people without remainder; they are fleeting, and, on occasion, they can seriously seek to disturb each other.[138] But they must not try to usurp each other's place. Of course, pools can also literally displace people by leaving no space for citizens to assemble – a charge levelled against the prominent reflecting pools in Albany's modernist Empire State Plaza in upstate New York, for instance.[139] But, in principle, they are one way in which architecture and spatial design might make the open-ended, and, yes, *uncertain*, character of democracy visible to citizens.

A critic might easily say that 'authorized assembly space' is just an insidious attempt to normalize or domesticate movements for protest or prefiguration. But the point remains that such spaces signal how comfortable a democracy is with rambunctious politics on squares, and, in general, people clamouring to articulate their second thoughts. In the mid-1960s the British architect Cedric Price designed a 'Pop-Up Parliament' meant to replace the Palace of Westminster. In his drawings Price included what he called a 'Rally Area'; it would have included floor heating and nylon coverings protecting protestors from rain, in addition to large screens showing the goings-on in Parliament on a tower supposed to replace Big Ben. Unlike with many government buildings surrounded by traffic or pools so large that the public has no place, and, unlike with so many of today's strict zoning laws, which signal that the public is primarily seen as a threat, Price's design would have told demonstrators 'you're most welcome'.[140] Brian Haw's ten years protesting in front of Parliament certainly would have been more comfortable.

People are not condemned to be completely helpless in the absence of such designs for public space. There can be creative uses of private spaces: think for instance of how, in the last years of Slobodan Milošević, citizens of Belgrade went out onto their balconies when the news started on television and banged pots and pans to drown out the state's propaganda. (Such noise-making – with no special equipment needed – is known in Latin America as *cacerolazo*; it has a long tradition there.)

Privately owned public spaces (POPS) can also have uses that their owners never imagined. Recall Zuccotti Park, the major site of Occupy Wall Street; unlike city-owned green spaces, Zuccotti initially had no rules against pitching tents. After 2017, the atrium of Trump Tower, of all places, became the staging ground for a weekly reading by a protestor; giving the public access to the atrium had been the price for Trump's company adding extra floors. (People generally know about the atrium; few know that gardens up in the Tower are also meant to be open to the public, at least during shopping hours.)

These instances of repurposing privately owned public space do not invalidate the point that a state, by creating or, for that matter, not creating public space for protest and prefiguration is sending a message to its citizens. From this perspective, it is remarkable that the space in front of London's City Hall is owned by Kuwait's sovereign wealth fund; not surprisingly, it comes with plenty of restrictions.[141] Quite apart from that message, there is also the fact that 'POPOS' – 'privately owned public open spaces' – can easily be rendered inhospitable (taking away benches, for instance, or putting large plants on them), and that their rules are often not clearly codified; and that security personnel might unevenly apply whatever exists by way of rules. (They always seemed to find reasons to deny access to the gardens in Trump Tower for the very few who even knew about them.)[142] One is ultimately at the mercy of people who have no public mandate – and who are difficult to make accountable to the public.

One may well have doubts whether, after the insurrection at the US Capitol on 6 January 2021, the metaphor of the siege should not be taken out of circulation. To have a chance of rescuing that image (and encouraging citizens not to shy away from their representatives), we need to say more about the institutions that can become the target of a siege, which is to say: legislatures – sometimes considered 'palaces of the people'.

2

Palace: Houses of the People, for the People, by the People?

Our buildings, above all the public buildings, ought in some fashion to be poems. And the images they offer to our senses must excite in us sentiments analogous to the functions to which the buildings are devoted.

Étienne-Louis Boullée

. . . and we said let's create 'public space' in the building, make it the most transparent TV station in the world . . .

Rem Koolhaas on building the CCTV centre in Beijing

Just before Christmas 2020, in the dying days of his first administration, Donald Trump took time off from his busy schedule promoting the Big Lie about having won the election and preparing fraudulent slates of electors to help him hold on to power: he found occasion to issue an executive order entitled 'Promoting Beautiful Federal Civic Architecture'. The order made 'classicism' the preferred style for new federal buildings, stopping just short of banning modernism entirely.[1] This aesthetic intervention – justified in the name of 'beauty', like many things Trump said and did, or at

CCTV in Beijing: '. . . and we said let's create 'public space' in the building, make it the most transparent TV station in the world . . .'.

least pretended to do – came with a larger set of prescriptions as to how US history ought to be understood: the President's '1776 Commission' mandated a singularly correct reading of the American past, to be fed directly into patriotic education across the country.[2]

The man who built plenty of other 'palaces' around the world and in the United States, including 'Trump Palace' on the Upper East Side, did not then get to realize his vision of federal architecture. In fact, plenty of his own buildings had never been particularly classical, but rather modern on the outside, and a nouveau-riche fever fantasy of Versailles, or what one astute critic called 'regional car dealership rococo', on the inside.[3] What's more, Trump's supporters ended up significantly damaging an existing classical edifice during the insurrection at the Capitol on 6 January 2021.[4]

As so often in Trump's first term, the grandiose gesture about architecture felt more like wanting to put a prop in place for the sake of instant consumption by the public, as opposed to any kind of long-term plan: the president frequently used cartoonish images – seemingly made for TV audiences – to convince people that something important had happened: in January 2017 an enormous pile of papers had 'proved' that the real-estate developer had properly divested from his business; in 2020 another pile demonstrated conclusively that there really existed a 'beautiful' health-care plan. And so on. The slapdash Commission report – and vague visions of Greek- and Roman-looking buildings – was supposed to prove that the United States had always been, and could still be, a proper and proud democracy (and not, let's say, a polity inextricably linked to legacies of slavery). At the time of writing, the Commission report remains buried in the archive, but a new executive order in favour of classical building styles was issued on day one of Trump's second term. Nine months later the East Wing was torn down, with a view to constructing a large ballroom in classical style.[5]

These episodes leave us with difficult questions as to what 'palaces', or other building types for that matter, democracy might plausibly feature in. Historically, plenty of democratic, or at least proto-democratic, legislatures have simply occupied existing ones designed for very different purposes: Westminster is a former church; the French National Assembly sits in what had been an aristocratic palace, as does the French Senate; the Taiwanese Legislative Yuan occupies a former all-girls high school; the first post-war West German parliament met in an academy for teacher-training; until May 2023, India's Lokh Sabha, the lower house of its bicameral parliament, convened in an edifice created by and for the Raj.

From time to time new buildings become necessary or possible: Westminster burnt down in 1834; a fire had started in the House of Lords; after the tumultuous years of the French Revolution, the state would have had enough money to build new housing for the National Assembly (but it never did); German members of parliament kept complaining so much that their chamber felt like a university where they were being lectured at from on high[6] (one of the parliament's presidents, Christian Democrat Richard Stücklen, also missed 'splendour') that an architect was tasked with designing a new chamber; the spaces for the Indian parliament were considered too small. And in Africa, just in the last two decades, China has built or refurbished more than fifteen parliament buildings; all expenses are covered, subsequent maintenance is included. (In fact, it has to be included, since only Chinese engineers have the relevant know-how: the dome of Malawi's parliament is now being repaired each year by Chinese contractors.)[7]

In moments of apparent tabula rasa, with the possibility of architectural, and, in particular, stylistic resets, the question becomes acute: what should a democratic 'palace' – a term regularly used in such debates – look like?

The word palace goes back to a specific place: the Palatine Hill in Rome. There, emperors were competing to erect magnificent private residences that also had administrative functions; at the same time they continued the tradition of creating or at least embellishing forums to commemorate military triumphs. Helmut Kohl's minister for housing liked to quote a line from Pliny the Younger to his boss – 'The Caesar must build' – encouraging a grander Chancellery.[8] Originally, the imperative referred not just to self-glorification and projecting power across society, but also the need to gain the support of subjects through eminently useful projects: Caesars, from Julius to Napoleon, self-declared successor to the Roman emperors, also brought water and sewage systems to cities.

There is every reason why democracies should improve the built environment for all. But do they also have to build a type of *palatium* – edifices that, historically, were not just combining private residence and administrative offices,[9] but also served as manifestations of social hierarchy, and that, one would think, were designed to keep the people at a distance?[10] Not for nothing does the world's most influential absolute monarch reside in an edifice known as the Apostolic Palace.

Ludwig Wittgenstein held that architecture serves only to glorify, and one can understand why new parliaments in the nineteenth century hoped to gain prestige by presenting themselves as palaces.[11] What exactly is it that a democratic architecture should glorify though? The citizenry itself? Does that require a problematic image of a single, homogeneous people – a Hercules – when in fact the people are never one, but can only appear in the plural?[12] Or should one perhaps glorify a set of procedures? Contrary to what is sometimes asserted, democratic procedures are *not* entirely invisible: they are codified somewhere; and citizens, and especially professional politicians, can be observed following them; like other rituals, they affirm the character of the polity. But can such ideas somehow be translated into an iconographic programme for buildings serving democratic purposes? When the parliament in Budapest opened in 1902, the architect Imre Steindl called what was at the time the largest legislative assembly in the world a 'Temple of the Constitution'. It is doubtful that anyone at the time understood the edifice as quite such a thing; although its admirers would have noticed that the Gothic style and its location next to the Danube evoked Westminster – very much in line with what Hungarian liberals saw as a parallel between their past and a British Whig tradition.

So: does democracy have an inherent image problem? Let's revisit and expand the observation that John Quincy Adams made in 1831:

> Democracy has no forefathers, it looks to no posterity; it is swallowed up in the present, and thinks of nothing but itself. This is the vice of Democracy, and it is incurable. Democracy has no monuments. It strikes no medals. It bears the head of no man on a coin; its very essence is iconoclastic.[13]

The argument was put forward by a deeply embittered politician, someone disenchanted by democracy and therefore perhaps prone to claiming that democracy could never be enchanted. But the thought would also appear to render implausible even a much more self-critical approach to national histories of democracy, for instance in the form of a political pedagogy along the lines of: *this*, future generations should understand, is what our fundamental political commitments as a country are; and, deviating from the uncritical stance of Trump's ill-fated Commission: this is how and why we have failed to achieve our ideals so far, and must try harder. For, according to Adams, democracy is not just impotent as a symbol-maker; it is also incapable of giving an account of its past and its future.

The United States has evidently not followed Adams's line of reasoning: it has plenty of heads of men, and rarely, women, on coins and dollar notes. It keeps creating grand monuments even when other democracies have long opted for a more abstract, or even self-effacing, approach (to this day, though, there is no monument to Adams). But these are just facts; they do not by themselves answer the question about democracy's proper self-representation. Are doubts here ultimately animated by a fear of the concrete and an anxiety of embodiment that, perversely, might result in a weakening of democracies, as democrats are left speechless – and imageless – in the face of Trumpian (or smarter authoritarians') visions of 'beauty'?

I suggest breaking the question of 'democratic palaces' down into four parts: first, the relationship of democracy to monuments, which, on the most basic level, is a means to draw attention and signal where a polity seeks to invest its resources. Thomas Jefferson, for instance, desired the Capitol to be 'a durable and honorable monument to our infant republic'.

Second, there is the long-standing discussion whether democracy might be associated with particular styles and materials, as in: classicism is Rome and Athens, and that's democracy; or another exceedingly conventional thought: glass is transparency and transparency is democracy. Here the question is about clothing, so to speak, not size.

Third, and on a related note: ought democracy to come with a particular iconographic programme? We already saw how the Athenians placed statues glorifying the Tyrannicides

Harmodios and Aristogeiton prominently in the agora – as exemplars of democratic action. But should contemporary democracies venerate individuals in such ways?

Finally, and, as I will suggest, most important: what types of rooms should buildings devoted to democracy provide? As we already saw, spaces do not simply determine human behaviour, but behaviour can re-codify the meaning of spaces; yet saying that answers are complicated here does not make the question meaningless, nor does it imply that any answer is as good as any other. One plausible answer, it will turn out, was given by Louis Kahn with his parliament building in Dhaka.

Should Democracy Build in a Monumental Manner?

On a very basic level, the investment in conspicuous public buildings signals the importance that a collective assigns to particular functions.[14] At the risk of stating the obvious: size and height matter.[15] Kaiser Wilhelm II really did not want the cupola of the Reichstag – the parliament building he had grudgingly conceded to his subjects at the end of the nineteenth century and located just outside Berlin's city boundary – to be higher than that of his palace on Unter den Linden. (Whether the enormous size of the Reichsgericht in Leipzig indicated that the *Rechtsstaat* was valued more than any building associated with democracy is a question harder to answer; by contrast, it was a very conscious choice that today's Chancellery had to be fourteen metres lower than the parliament building.)

Then again, automatically associating size, and height in particular, with actual political significance is a risky manoeuvre. In some cases it's downright misleading: when what remains the world's second-largest (and heaviest) building was completed, it just sat there as an entirely powerless 'civic centre' – the Palatul Parlamentului in Bucharest in the 1980s.[16] More important still, since the totalitarian regimes of the twentieth century, there is the pervasive thought that monumentality might somehow in and of itself be undemocratic; it constitutes what the Germans call an *Überwältigungsarchitektur* – an architecture meant to overwhelm individuals.

Yet seminal thinkers on democracy sometimes came to the exact opposite conclusion: Tocqueville held that citizens in a democracy would be particularly attracted by monumentality. He observed that 'nowhere do citizens seem more insignificant than in a democratic nation. Nowhere

The view from the Berlin Chancellery to the Reichstag. The large empty space would have housed the Civic Forum.

does the nation seem greater or make a vaster impression on the mind.' He went on to claim that 'in democratic societies man's imagination shrinks when he thinks of himself as an individual and expands without limit when he thinks of the state. Hence the same men who live cramped in scant quarters often nurse gigantic ambitions when they turn their attention to public monuments.'[17] Thus, according to Tocqueville, 'democracy encourages men not just to produce a host of trifling works but also to erect a small number of very great monuments. Between these two extremes, however, there is nothing.'[18] In his lifetime Tocqueville could only ever think of one 'very great monument' built in more or less democratic circumstances: the long harbour wall in Cherbourg, not far from the town of Tocqueville itself.[19]

A century later, during a protracted debate about modernism and monumentality, some architectural theorists continued Tocqueville's line of reasoning. The Modernist Sigfried Giedion argued that 'monuments are human landmarks which men have created as symbols of their ideals, for their aims, and for their actions'; he went on to claim that 'the most vital monuments are those which express the feeling and thinking of this collective force – the people'.[20]

By contrast, Lewis Mumford categorically denied that there could be modern monumentality; he also highlighted what he saw as democracy's necessarily difficult relationship to monumentality – what Mumford diagnosed as democracy's 'grudging attitude' towards monuments. His argument had nothing to do with the fears of totalitarianism typical of the mid-twentieth century, though; rather, he claimed that a democracy would shy away from monumentality primarily because democratic governments were loath to spend vast resources on monuments, as opposed to schemes improving the day-to-day lives of citizens.[21] As Mumford put it, 'to raise all living standards to a decent level, at least to the "minimum of existence", is the aim of modern man: not to elevate and sanctify one side of life at the expense of every other aspect'.[22]

Whether that thought might explain the relatively small size of parliaments in some relatively Social Democratic countries – think Norway – is a matter of speculation. What's not is that countries eager to signal their distance from a totalitarian past consciously built in a modest manner, to the point of self-effacement.[23] Historically, such efforts coincided with the early Cold War period when the International Style was promoted as inherently 'free' and 'democratic', contrasting with a Stalinist approach that was gigantic, nationalistic, and baroque all at the same time. Bonn and Karlsruhe – seats of the West German government and of the country's constitutional court respectively – turned out to be prime examples of an architecture seeking to avoid even a hint of a totalitarian primacy of the political: when a new Chancellery was built in the 1970s, Helmut Schmidt likened it to the office of a local savings bank. And when the judges of the newly established post-Soviet Russian constitutional court came to visit, they could not believe that the German jurists were housed in a rather modest glass building – as opposed to the palace, former residence of the margraves and dukes of Baden, very nearby.

By contrast, in the mid-1970s, the East German government erected a monumental Palast der Republik in the middle of Berlin, on the very site where the Prussian royal palace had once stood. (In 1950, GDR leader Walter Ulbricht had ordered what remained of the palace after the Second World War to be blown to bits.) Ceaușescu brutally destroyed parts of Bucharest's old town and relocated 40,000 people to clear space for his sprawling Casa Poporului. These were icons of a supposed devotion to the people: edifices like the Palast der Republik not only housed the parliament, but also provided entertainment with dance halls, a bowling alley, bars and restaurants – all in the name of facilitating a classless, fraternal socialist way of life. The buildings, just like the infamous large housing projects, were to function as 'social condensers', spaces for creating a socialist people through the right kinds of continuous and informal social interactions.[24] Often, the people themselves could not reside in or even near the edifices meant to glorify them; they were relegated to cheap prefab high-rises far away from the palaces at the heart of capital cities. Put bluntly, the palatial self-representation of the political system was a lie.

People for sure think that size matters. The world's second largest building, Ceaușescu's Palace, on the left; on the right: the world's largest Orthodox Church.

Yet, as the German political theorist Herfried Münkler has pointed out, there is nothing necessarily democratic about *minimizing* the visibility of political authority.[25] Violence is easily visible; authority is not. Showing where political authority resides is prima facie preferable to effacing it; at the very least, it becomes a target for public attention, a focus of accountability, and possibly a site of protest. As we saw in the previous chapter, all kinds of regimes have created what Lefebvre called 'monumental space'. They all signalled with monumentality that something significant was happening in a particular place. By making themselves more visible, they also made themselves more vulnerable. And, as we saw, democracy in fact demands a certain kind of vulnerability: civic opposition needs to know where it needs to go.

Making authority visible and subject to sporadic protest will not necessarily render holders of authority accountable: visibility is not the same as what the British philosopher Onora O'Neill has called 'assessability', and that in turn is not the same as accountability.[26] True, what is successfully hidden can hardly become subject to political judgement. But visibility does not guarantee that one can truly assess matters of collective concern; even if one can assess them, further political mechanisms are required to make those exercising authority accountable.

None of this means that buildings in the service of democracy must overshadow everything else, or that they need to 'glorify'. A parliament just needs to be dignified, not glorified – in that sense, contrary to Frank Lloyd Wright's claim, as a distinctly democratic building, it's not really relaxed. What results from this is not an affirmation of Trumpian beauty, based on the idea that citizens will only read classical architecture (and an Oval Office decorated with fake golden ornaments) as projecting dignity; it's not true that only conventional forms are 'legible' to citizens. But it does follow that a building that matters for democracy should not be an indistinguishable office building. Schmidt had a point with his complaint.

So do critics of the architecture of the European Union: because of the haggling over the location of the different European institutions – primarily a tug-of-war between France, Belgium, and Luxembourg – and because, until 1992, the EU did not control or even finance its own buildings, the world's most important supranational experiment ended up with distinctly non-glorious edifices – some might say undignified ones. Belgium had the Berlaymont, the seat of the European Commission, built on spec: it resembled the UNESCO headquarters designed by Marcel Breuer and other modernists for Paris, but, in case the Commission did not stay in Brussels, it was also meant to be fit for use as a rather ordinary ministry or even a commercial office building. (In the end, the Eurocrats did not want open-plan offices; the hastily added partitions contained enormous amounts of asbestos, which eventually necessitated a thirteen-year renovation.) Because of French sensitivities over the location of the European Parliament – initially in Strasbourg – the Belgians tasked a twenty-six-year-old architect with creating what could only be referred to as an 'international conference centre' – but was intended as the Brussels seat of the Parliament (today the deputies divide their time between Brussels and Strasbourg).

The haphazard architecture – which has never generated memorable icons such as the White House – would seem to reflect a truth about the EU more broadly. Integration has not just been an ongoing (and opaque) process; it has not only been a matter of often unseemly (and opaque) compromises among national interests; it has also happened by stealth. One does not have to be a diehard Eurosceptic to suspect that the promoters of integration did not want to make the institutions too visible and thereby also render them more vulnerable; promoting the European flag and anthem already aroused enough suspicion that a superstate was being created. With the EU's architecture, the emphasis on process and everything being provisional – not necessarily undemocratic, if you think back to the idea of democracy as a politics of second thoughts – has entirely won out over the need to make authority easily recognizable (and, ultimately, accountable).

The exception is the building of the European Central Bank in Frankfurt. One could hardly have monetary union by stealth anyway, even if Adams's point about democracy – it 'bears the head of no man' – is in fact true of the single currency's banknotes. The Austrian architect Wolf Prix used a hyperboloid cut to make the ECB edifice – standing isolated from Frankfurt's commercial bank towers – a unique icon (except that he used a very similar design a few years later to win the competition for the Azeri central bank, reinforcing the suspicion that an EU building is always just another, not particularly special or even dignified, office building).[27] Still, the space outside the ECB is one of the rare sites where European citizens do go to protest against EU policies.

Why Would Anyone Want an 800-ton Glass Dome?

Plenty of political leaders have insisted that public buildings must exhibit a particular style, explicitly appealing to political, as opposed to aesthetic, considerations in the process. What they have often really meant is whatever they happened to consider a *national* style: legislatures, but also edifices housing the executive, are meant to express *national* traditions. Sir Christopher Wren observed that 'Architecture has its Political Use; publick Buildings being the Ornament of a Country; it establishes a Nation, draws People and Commerce.'[28] Goethe associated the German with the Gothic; he derided the French and Italians as epigones of the classical (eventually, Goethe himself was to convert to the classic).[29] British elites also pushed relentless pro-Gothic propaganda when debating whether Westminster ought to be rebuilt in the classical style after the Great Fire of 1666. Some worried that classicism, much discussed as an alternative at the time, was not only the style of supposed 'republican temples', but also a sign of revolutionary sentiments. 'It is one of the advantages of Gothic architecture,' claimed John Ruskin, that its 'minute and multitudinous sculptural decorations afford means of expressing, either symbolically or literally, all that need to be known of national feeling or achievement.'[30]

Today, theorists of architecture are not particularly given to discussions of style. But laypeople are, for better or for worse, and when they do discuss style, they also tend to operate in the shadow of totalitarianism. For the very association of the classical with attractive political values was put into question in the twentieth century, as 'stripped classicism' became widely perceived as the signature style of National Socialism. Cartoonish images of megalomaniacal projects – most prominently Albert Speer's designs for the Volkshalle and Via Triumphalis in Berlin (neither were built) – remain firmly lodged in our political consciousness.

Yet this is a false collective memory, so to speak. Fascism adopted many architectural styles (and theories) – especially in Italy, where strands of modernism were promoted long after they had become officially condemned in Nazi Germany. Even in the Third Reich, what actually got built – as opposed to Speer's monstrous plans for Berlin – was a mixture of monumentality, 'the classical' (as Speer himself liked to put it), and the modern: a 'monumentalized modernity'.[31] A similar style and, for that matter, somewhat similar spaces, were created in the dwindling number of democracies in the 1930s, invoking ideals of collective mastery over history: looked at from a bit of distance, the edifice of the Federal Reserve in Washington, DC, can easily be imagined as the office building dealing with monetary policy in a thousand-year *Reich*.

Nazi architecture certainly did seek to overwhelm; it also, less obviously, promoted a kind of uniformity through over-long rows of windows and arcades that appear to leave the viewer with no possibility to establish an individual hold on the edifice – unlike Gothic cathedrals which might also overwhelm, but which, through their individual masonry and ornaments, allow the single believer to find their own way of connecting with the building and worship (and then having their eyes pulled upward towards heaven).[32] The sheer mass of compact 'people material' assigned places inside and around enormous Nazi edifices were meant to reinforce the image of a homogeneous *Volksgemeinschaft* stripped of all individuality.

Fascist architecture sought to constrain viewers into adopting a particular perspective and focus on the leader holding forth, usually from a balcony. After the end of Italian Fascism, Rome's Palazzo Venezia, where Mussolini had had his office – and his balcony – featured a banner saying 'Basta con i Balconi!'[33] Austria has never re-opened what came to be known as the 'Hitler-Balkon', technically a terrace at the centre of Vienna's Hofburg Palace; from there in March 1938 the Führer had declared the Anschluss to 200,000 enthusiastic Austrians assembled on Heldenplatz (Heroes' Square). Only one person ever gave a speech from that space after 1938: the political activist and Holocaust survivor Elie Wiesel, who said that the balcony itself meant nothing and that a change in political culture would have to come from the people below, not from the balcony.

What makes the most obvious difference between these edifices and buildings like Senate House in London or some of the enormous 'republican temples' built in Washington, DC, in the interwar period? The fascist iconographic programme, most notably a cult of future sacrifice and glorified death that had no equivalent in the democracies at the time (or since, for that matter): the Nazis, after all, sought to build memorials for the war dead *in advance* of military combat, in addition to a triumphal arch more than twice as high as Napoleon's Arc de Triomphe and inscribed with the names of 1.8 million Germans killed in the First World War.[34]

If fascist architecture foreshadowed war, military edifices and war materials must have been central to Fascism's approach to building.[35] That partly explains the intuition behind fashioning supposedly democratic architecture out of glass, for no fortress can be made of such material; and no warriors will want to be on full display (and Hitler apparently hated glass as a material).[36] Glass is habitually said to signal 'transparency' as a supposedly core democratic feature, a tendency particularly strong in West Germany in the post-war period: politicians connected the notion of democracy to the public, the notion of the public to the idea of porousness, and porousness to transparency, as ensured by glass.[37] Konrad Adenauer proved the exception: he implored Hans Schwippert, the architect who redesigned the teachers' academy in Bonn to house the parliament, not to have large windows; it reminded Adenauer of what he thought was a 'horrible' building by Le Corbusier, made entirely of glass and iron, he supposedly had seen in Geneva.[38] But, in general, the assumption went: if Hitler's *Wort aus Stein* had read 'dictatorship', then after 1945 a West German state's *Wörter aus Glass* automatically spelled 'democracy'.

Yet lack of transparency is hardly the most striking characteristic of totalitarianism; in fact, given that all know that all eyes ought to be on the leader, it could be seen as oddly transparent. What's more, totalitarianism sought to create spectacles in which totalitarian subjects were all supposed to be visible to each other – albeit not in their individual differences, of course, only as forming a homogeneous collective actor following a given script. Eerily reminiscent, in fact, of Rousseau's ideal festival modelled on a male regiment.

Mussolini once declared: '*il fascismo è una casa di vetro in cui tutti possono guardare*' – Fascism is a house made of glass into which all can look. This statement found literally concrete expression in one of the most remarkable buildings constructed during the 'twenty black years' in Italy: Giuseppe Terragni's Casa del Fascio in Como. Terragni's cube featured large glass windows and doors, suggesting a seamless connection between the fascist people and their representatives on the inside; it also had ingenious openings to the sky and Fascist party offices open to the large atrium. Lest there be any doubt, Terragni himself announced: 'Here is the Mussolinian concept that Fascism is a glass house into which everyone can peer, giving rise to the architectural interpretation that is the complement of this idea: no encumbrance, no barrier, no obstacle between the political hierarchy and the people.'[39] To illustrate his point, Terragni published montages of his building at the centre of a Fascist rally, the edifice entirely enveloped by the masses in black.

While by all accounts modernist in style and a prime example of Italian *razionalismo* – a Nazi *Rationalismus* would have been unthinkable – the Casa del Fascio was also cleverly inserted into Como to suggest a continuity with the Roman Empire; Terragni effectively created a vertical version of the Roman *castrum*, while alluding to a combination of later elements of Italian architecture, such as the *torre del commune* and the Renaissance assembly hall (all the while also confronting – some might think, directly opposing – the baroque church in the centre of Como).[40]

As Terragni's own montage with the masses – purely imaginary, there never was such a rally – suggested, Mussolini's imperative to create a glass house for Fascism meant that the people would relate to Fascism as a spectacle of power: the building was as much a temple and a monument as it was an office building, or, for that matter, a house open to and

Como's Casa del Fascio: The realization of Mussolini's idea that fascism is a house made of glass into which all can look?

for the people. The impression of the Casa as really temple-cum-monument was strengthened by the edifice's iconographic programme: a statue of the Duce (who, by the way, was also occasionally depicted as Hercules), and an unplastered, visibly damaged concrete column (behind glass!) in the middle of the office of the *segretario generale* was supposed to invoke the heroic street fighting of the *squadristi*.[41]

One building hardly proves that the intuitions behind West Germany's post-war architecture of and for transparency were mistaken.[42] And there seems to have been no problem with Terragni's edifice after the war when it was simply renamed the Casa del Popolo (today, it houses the Guardia di Finanza – and remains a pilgrimage site for architects from all over the world). But there was also no problem when Oscar Niemeyer's new headquarters of the French Communist Party, located in the working-class area of Belleville in Paris and opened in 1971, was touted as a *maison de verre*, even though the facade was actually reflecting and thus did not allow anyone to look inside, and even though no one thought of Communist parties as particularly transparent.[43]

The real point is this: visibility does not ensure actual comprehension; and comprehension remains powerless without the means of political participation. There is a very long way from 'seeing' to political accountability, with many arduous steps in between. The step from seeing to understanding would appear the least difficult. And yet: glass can also mirror; it's not automatically transparent. What's more, actual, total transparency – all is truly visible – might be a particularly effective tool of obfuscation. Overwhelming audiences with information allows one to claim that everyone can 'see' everything; but it might take a long time to comprehend what any piece of information means, and how all the pieces of information fit together.

What lies behind glass might be fully visible, but the objects themselves can remain opaque, an analogy to situations in which the need to satisfy an audience hankering after transparency leads people to make up things they know will be acceptable – just not entirely true.[44] Last but not least, glass might suggest some kind of honesty – you see what you get. You might, as Susan Sontag once remarked apropos 'transparence', experience 'things being what they are'; what's more, glass might give the impression of *equality*, at least in the sense of a very basic reciprocity: we see them; they see us.[45] But glass also separates; the separation becomes visible only in the moment when glass is shattered – which also puts into doubt the notion that the Casa del Fascio both symbolized and enabled the 'immediate' relationship between the leader and the masses. Those inside were privileged (and protected); and they decided who was granted entry.[46]

To state the obvious: how politics actually functions can never just be simply read off visual orders, stylistic choices, or, for that matter, the deployment of particular materials. West German politics did not become more transparent because Schwippert insisted on large windows (he also imagined that, with windows open in warmer months, citizens could just listen in); nor is Norman Foster's famed 'transparent' dome atop the Reichstag in Berlin – built at the insistence of German politicians who rejected Foster's initial design of a glass and steel canopy spanning the nineteenth-century building – proof that the politics of unified Germany is more comprehensible, let alone more accessible, to its citizens.

True, the sovereign, or at least a small selection of the sovereign, that is the citizens inside the dome, are placed *on top* of their representatives. The same type of gesture exists in Canberra, where Australians can walk on top of a grassy hill into which the parliament – lauded as highly democratic when it was opened in 1988 – had been built. Yet that gesture can feel a tad arbitrary: in the Scottish Parliament, one of the most remarkable political edifices of the post-war period, the people enter the building *underneath* the chamber, in a rather dark, vaulted room with saltire flags on the concrete ceiling above them; they are said to be 'carrying' or supporting democracy like columns (or so at least explained the Parliament's 'Visitor Services Manager' who graciously showed me around).

In Berlin the gesture also feels a little ironic in light of the fact that, legally, Germany usually keeps the sovereign people as a collective actor safely at a distance: referendums at the federal level are prohibited. If anything, citizens and tourists ascending the ramps inside the cupola become a spectacle for each other, with little connection to the inaudible, and for the most part actually invisible, political goings-on far below. What most likely will attract their attention is the unparalleled view over the capital city, rather than a vaguely felt presence of politics beneath them.[47]

A not even particularly cynical observer might say that the Reichstag dome does not lie; it tells the truth about how we are distracted from common concerns by spectacles, including tourist ones. None of this has prevented the dome from becoming a model; Bulgarians, seeking to construct a new parliament, considered imitating the dome, as did architects charged with replacing the current edifice of the Russian Duma, characterized by what two acerbic critics describe as 'a hybrid of 1970s Soviet stagnation chic and 1990s restrained bureaucratic bling'.[48]

Never mind truths and lies of different buildings, though; even the underlying assumption that parliamentary politics specifically should be as transparent as possible is wrong. A fully transparent parliament is probably a largely powerless one; there is no need for difficult committee negotiations and the hard work of compromises behind closed doors, because what parties, or even individual deputies, think and want is irrelevant in the first place.[49]

'Seeing through' as a political demand and glass as material are not the only possible understandings of transparency, however. György Kepes, a theorist associated with the New Bauhaus in Chicago, suggested we think of transparency very differently: as an overlapping without obscuring, as 'interpenetration without optical destruction'. This is a matter of organizing objects and spatial relations, as opposed to the qualities of one material. The literal kind of transparency is relatively easy to achieve in architecture; the organizational kind requires careful, mostly modernist, design.[50]

This conception might still invite the objections I just levelled against the customary transparency kitsch: a system of divided powers, or checks and balances, might also aim at 'interpenetration without destruction', but the spatial relations among different buildings devoted to different powers – think of the Praça dos Três Poderes in Brasília, declared to be 'the Versailles of the People' by its designer Lúcio Costa – do not explain how the powers actually interact. 'Interpenetration' also in no way ensures wider political participation. Again, one cannot jump from recognizing a particular material or reading a visual order and safely land on the firm ground of political knowledge. Or legal knowledge, for that matter: in Georgia, after years of flagrant corruption, the government decided to construct new police stations – out of glass. Transparency International, the well-known organization fighting corruption, lauded that design choice. Apparently, petty corruption indeed went down; larger-scale, systemic corruption, not so much.

Icons of Democracy?

If an iconographic programme can make the difference between a fascist building and a democratic building, we need to determine if there is a clear and distinct iconography of democracy. As we saw, John Quincy Adams denied that there could be such a thing. Democracy is about the people as a collective actor, but differences, even conflicts, within the collective are – on all plausible understandings of democracy – legitimate. The king is *one*, and his two bodies – the physical one and the body politic – can be represented as unitary;[51] democracy might need embodiments, but certainly no single body can ever represent a democratic body politic as such (even if there is an official head of state).

Those instituting democracy in the modern world – most obviously the French Revolutionaries – suffered intense anxieties about the polity's lack of unity. One solution was to ensure unity through rituals: after a majority vote in the National Assembly, ballots were burnt and a unanimous decision was staged as the final, official one.[52] Festivals where citizens watched *each other*, rather than passively consume official performances, held out the promise of deepening fraternal feelings. As we saw in the last chapter, these elaborate *fêtes* revisited the central locations of the Revolution; they concluded on open fields where the people, or so it was hoped, could experience themselves as a fully united collective, with attention focused on 'altars of the fatherland', 'liberty trees', and individuals drinking milk from gigantic statues of Isis. Of course, the entire nation could not see itself – but everyone might be able to do the same thing at exactly the same time. Simultaneity replaced visibility as the key to a ritual transformation; people could not all be in the same place, but, at least in theory, they could all think about the same thing at a given moment.[53]

Did the French people enjoy this? We do not really know. Did it work? We know it was deemed largely unsuccessful. In the course of the 1790s, republican festivals in France became dominated by military parades; any unchoreographed interaction among citizens was de-emphasized in favour of spectacles that stressed the new Republic's strength, especially vis-à-vis outside powers who posed a permanent threat to the democratic experiment unfolding in the country. Instead of the processions, held nationwide at the same time, Louis-Marie de La Révellière-Lépeaux, a deputy to the National Convention and later a member of the Directory, proposed a giant amphitheatre around an altar of the fatherland (never built): a select group of passive spectators instead of the people as a whole acting simultaneously.

All the while, attempts to render the Republic, and the people for that matter, legible in the form of a single symbol proved unsuccessful: as we saw, statues of Hercules were proposed by radical revolutionaries who considered Marianne, the national allegorical symbol of the French Republic representing Liberty, Equality, and Fraternity, somehow too moderate; when that idea proved too abstract, Voltaire himself (according to Louis XVI, singularly responsible for the misery of the Revolution, alongside Rousseau) was presented as Hercules.[54] In the tumultuous year 1848 another festival was staged on what today is called the Place de la Concorde; people scoffed at things like the Chariot of Agriculture and an unfinished Colossus embodying the Republic; Tocqueville remarked that the military parade had been the only serious part of the festival (which the art historian T. J. Clark was to dub a 'festival of obedience').[55] Subsequently, a grand competition was held to find the Republic's definitive female figuration. Seven hundred painters participated, receiving vague instructions that she should be portrayed as seated, to signal that republican politics meant stability. The public responded with mockery; art critics recommended that some of the painters should look for another profession. Eventually, the search for the one unifying symbol was abandoned altogether.[56]

Still, republican *festomanie*, intended to imbue spaces with political values and teach the people democratic *moeurs*, lived on. Contrary to the view that the Weimar Republic suffered from a deficit in political symbolism (and hence emotional support), the Republic – after some initial reluctance – invested massively in large ceremonies celebrating the constitution, arguably the most progressive of its time; it also sought to coin medals and it erected monuments – in short, all the things Adams thought democracy couldn't do.[57] The Republic even devoted resources to the design of stamps, with the learned assistance of legendary art historian Aby Warburg, who thought stamps could be of global political importance.[58]

The monuments – to foreign minister Gustav Stresemann, for example – were abstract; some festivities, like the much-promoted Goethe anniversary in 1932, had little obvious connection to democracy; and many spectacular ideas were never realized – such as Hugo Häring's plan to erect enormous stands in front of the Reichstag, from which citizens were supposed to have observed their representatives. Given that the parliamentary building did not even have the pseudo-transparency of Foster's dome, it is very hard to, well, see, how this was to have worked in practice.

Efforts to cultivate a democratic sensibility through the built environment – what the Republic's *Reichskunstwart* Robert Redslob called 'unconscious aesthetic education' – were deeply objectionable for the Nazis; they embarked on the systematic destruction of the Republic's monuments, including one designed by Mies van der Rohe, made of brick and dedicated to Communist martyrs Rosa Luxemburg and Karl Liebknecht. The Nazis spread their fascist iconoclasm across Europe: monuments devoted to French republicanism in Paris were wrecked systematically, as were sculptures designating enemies of *la République*: the reptiles – symbols of reactionary forces – at the bottom of the female figure towering over the Place de la République would disappear forever.[59]

We appear to be coming away from our inquiry empty-handed: there is no uniquely democratic style, let alone a uniquely democratic material; and there appears to be no particular democratic iconography. Does that mean democracies are bereft of visual strategies to reinforce support for them? A brief detour via a phenomenon that *appears* close to democracy – but is in the last instance hostile to it – might help: populism.

Populist Building Strategies, or:
The Double Movement

Conventional wisdom has it that, in the early twenty-first century, we are seeing an increasing number not only of populist parties and movements, but of regimes that can plausibly be called populist. Populism – contrary to what many pundits and politicians tend to claim – is not a matter of 'criticizing elites' or 'being angry at the establishment'; in fact, keeping a close eye on the powerful can be a civic virtue, as opposed to a sign of being a populist who somehow poses a danger to democracy. What is distinctive about populists is their claim that they, and *only they*, represent what they often refer to as 'the real people'.[60] This implies that all other contenders for power simply do not represent the people – because, so populists charge, all other politicians are fundamentally corrupt. At stake here is never just a disagreement about policies, or even one about values – after all, such conflicts are completely normal and ideally even productive in a democracy. Rather, populists make differences with others immediately *personal* and wholly a matter of *morality*: the others are never just misguided about policy or hold objectionable values; they are ultimately just bad, nefarious characters. Populists, on a basic level, deny the legitimacy of their political opponents.

Less obviously, the claim to a monopoly of representing the people also implies that all those citizens who do not share – or simply will not fit into – the ultimately symbolic construction of 'the people' undertaken by populists do not belong to the people at all. Populists always seek to exclude particular others. This happens obviously at the level of party politics; less obviously, but much more dangerously for democracy, at the level of the people themselves: there usually already vulnerable minorities are cast out from 'the real people'.

Note that this pattern of anti-pluralism does not commit populists to particular policies. But it does do one thing: it requires them to specify who the 'real people' are. And one underappreciated result of this requirement is that populists in power – if they have sufficient time and resources – seek to make their 'correct' understanding of the real people permanent in the built environment.[61] They do so through monumentality, through stylistic choices, and through particular iconographies.[62]

Recep Tayyip Erdoğan has had new mosques built all over Turkey, including the enormous Grand Çamlıca Mosque in Istanbul, which can accommodate more than 60,000 worshippers, and is visible from virtually anywhere in the city. A large mosque is also what those leaving the gigantic new airport will see first. In 2020 the president converted the Hagia Sophia from a museum into a mosque, releasing the building, as he put it, from 'chains of captivity'.[63] Not by accident did he pray at Hagia Sophia the day before the first round of presidential elections in 2023.

Viktor Orbán's enormously expensive reconstruction of Budapest's Castle District – making it the seat of government, replacing cultural institutions such as the National Gallery – evokes a late nineteenth-century bourgeois 'Golden Age'. The Habsburg-era buildings, while claiming to be 'faithful' to the originals, are often being created from photographs and in effect feature ornamentation around a concrete structure, similar to Erdoğan's mosques: what claims to be truly traditional is often postmodern pastiche; and, while heavily surveilled and guarded by police, these spaces also offer plenty of opportunities for consumption primarily aimed at tourists.

Even more telling is the redesign of the square around Hungary's parliament, what is often referred to as *nemzet főtere*, the main national square. The space has been restored to its condition in 1944, with a monument to Lajos Kossuth erected under state socialism replaced by the copy of an earlier monument that depicted the governor-president and national hero of the unsuccessful 1848 revolution against the Habsburgs as a rather downtrodden and isolated figure. An iconography condemning the 'red terror' after the First World War has also been restored, including a female statue glowering at the parliament building – after all, it was liberal parliamentarians, according to the right-wing reading of interwar history, that enabled the Communists to come to power. A statue of Mihály Károlyi, the liberal prime minister who had signed the Armistice after the First World War, had already been removed in 2012; later on, a memorial to Imre Nagy, leader of the ill-fated revolution of 1956, standing midway on a bridge, also disappeared. The restoration of the pre-1944 national square sends one clear signal: proper Hungarian history stopped with the occupation by Nazi Germany in March 1944; the state socialist period also does not properly belong to it. It is only in 2010 – the beginning of Orbán's second period as prime minister – that national history resumes. Meanwhile, despite what could charitably be understood as a gesture towards authenticity – everything has to be as before March 1944 – new elements have been added: an underground memorial to the villages and cities lost after the Treaty of Trianon in 1920, as a result of which Hungary had to give up about two-thirds of its territory after the First World War.

The reconstruction boom is not only a matter of nostalgia. Substantive stylistic choices are being made, and these judgements are linked to political ideology. Modernism and, in particular, the 'International Style', are derided by many populists as both overly rationalist, colonialist, or objectionably 'cosmopolitan', and 'rootless'. Some – from the Dutch far-right political entrepreneur Thierry Baudet to Trump – have made a point of condemning it as simply 'ugly'; Baudet, who has crafted an image as an intellectual-cum-dandy in politics, has also let it be known that aesthetics is more important than ethics.[64]

Just as we resisted the temptation to designate a particular style as democratic, it would be wrong to categorize any particular style as inherently populist. However, there's no doubt that some populist leaders have promoted particular styles as part of solidifying an understanding of 'the real people' – most obvious in the case of Erdoğan's choice of the Ottoman-Seljuk style.[65] Note how this is not just generally about 'nationalism' (Erdoğan's main opponents, the Kemalists, are nationalists, too, after all); rather, it is about cementing a particular notion of peoplehood in competition with other conceptions – and demonstrating the efficacy, or sheer power, of a regime in remaking a country in light of that anti-pluralist conception.

Note that these populist strategies benefit from plausible deniability. They are monumental, but they're not products of a personality cult; they do not immediately reveal themselves as propaganda. What one might call an imperative of 'Don't make it too obvious!' also applies to the comprehensive refashioning of New Delhi's Central Vista. Prime Minister Narendra Modi's favourite architect, fellow Gujarati Bimal Patel, has redesigned the large spaces in front of the government buildings created by Edward Lutyens and Herbert Baker in the last decades of the British Raj. Rather than replacing these edifices, new ones are being built next to them. In particular, a large triangular parliament has been erected right opposite the old circular one (what under the Raj had been the Council House); while new offices are also being created along what often reminds visitors of the Washington Mall. Changes are being justified in a decidedly technocratic language: better air conditioning; underpasses and proper bridges, better lighting, clean, well-kept lawns, parking, more toilets – very much in line with one aspect of Modi's self-presentation as a promoter of business and technological innovation. Other elements are more politically charged: for instance, what used to be known as the Rajpath – the architectural historian Kenneth Frampton called it a 'Baroque vista opening onto an empire that was already on the edge of being lost' – has been renamed the Kartavya Path, the road of duty.[66]

The new parliament was opened by Modi in May 2023 (opposition parties objected to the fact that the prime minister, not the country's president, was conducting the opening ceremony; twenty opposition parties boycotted the event entirely); other new buildings are still under construction, including a new office for the prime minister. It seems a fair guess, though, that none of them will make Modi's commitment to Hindutva – the core of his right-wing populism which leaves all non-Hindus, but especially Muslims, outside the conception of the 'real people' – too obvious. After all, this commitment is much more plausibly realized in the construction of Hindu temples (and the demolition of mosques).

The general pattern at the heart of the populist strategy is this, then: one layer of history is removed and a supposed reconstruction is celebrated as a return to popular authenticity and greatness: a process also very evident in Ayodhya, the supposed birthplace of Ram, where Hindu nationalists destroyed the Babri Masjid mosque in 1992 and where now the Ram Mandir (temple) is being built – completing the latter has been one of the major promises of Modi's Bharatiya Janata Party. The temple is not finished, but it was inaugurated by Modi in January 2024, in time for the national parliamentary elections; Modi performed religious rituals himself on that occasion.

A double movement of erasure and reconstruction takes different forms: with Modi, it means erasing mosques that had been built on top of Hindu temples – the idea is that the Mogul period is deleted; with Orbán, it means eradicating the modernist architecture associated with state socialism; in Erdoğan's case, the displacement of Kemalist modernist edifices by Islamic architecture, or at least buildings in appropriate Ottoman-Seljuk style, is the priority. The content differs. The anti-pluralist gesture is the same.

Where erasure is not possible, the second-best move, one might say, is diminishment. Think back to Bucharest's parliament building. For many reasons, some practical, some political, erasure is not an option; but somehow relativizing the edifice might be. Relativizing the world's second-largest building? The answer, it turns out, is an enormous Orthodox church built inside the area housing the parliament and enclosed by a wall.

Counter-Monuments, Anti-Monuments

Populism, then, is anti-pluralist; democracy, by contrast, is bound to be pluralist. It is so in terms of how it conceives of the people, and in its inner workings. Its complex set of ideals is difficult to render in any single symbolic condensation; monarchy and autocracy, on the other hand, can always fall back on the portrayal of a single person. It is not that democracy is without authority; but, unlike authoritarian regimes, it can question its own authority. Contrary to Adams's dire predictions, democracy will not bring down all statues. But, in recent years, plenty of statues *have* been brought down because who and, especially, what was represented could no longer possibly be seen as a legitimate object of veneration: colonialism and more or less subtle endorsements of the American old slave-holding South, to name only the most obvious.

Removal is not the only possibility, though. There are ways to contextualize and to create transparency in Kepes's sense of keeping different elements in view, establishing relations without 'optical destruction'. Rather than just removing a street name, it can be left in place, but disowned by a polity and complemented with a new sign featuring a new name, and an explanation of the change.[67] A street sign in Berlin's upper-class Grunewald district long featured the name Wissmann – for decades, nobody seemed to notice that Hermann von Wissmann had been the (particularly brutal) governor of Deutsch-Ostafrika, what today is Rwanda, Burundi, and Tanzania. The street's name was eventually changed to Barasch, honouring a Jewish couple who had lived in the street; in the working-class area of Neukölln, yet another Wissmannstrasse became Lucy-Lameck-Strasse, referring to the first female Tanzanian politician to hold a ministerial position. Such strategies of raising awareness of the past beyond the simplistic choice of glorification or destruction might be complemented online, allowing citizens to move between physical and virtual spaces.

Written explanations might seem overly pedagogical, perhaps even pedantic; what if an artistic object can subsume, or outright subvert, recognizable icons – prompting reflection about original and substitute, with veneration in either case? A statue like Kehinde Wiley's *Rumors of War* 'attempts to use the language of equestrian portraiture to both embrace and subsume the fetishisation of state violence', or so Wiley himself claimed. His man on horseback was a young African American with ripped jeans and sneakers. The statue was put in Times Square for two months and eventually moved to a permanent home in Richmond, Virginia, close to the infamous Monument Avenue where plenty of Confederate statues once stood.

A more radical approach still is state-approved vandalism: a vandalized statue that remains in place is both the original and a substitute that neither erases history nor allows for any kind of unreflective appropriation of it.[68] Here democracy might be iconoclastic, after all, but, for iconoclasm to be truly effective, something has to remain in place to make the iconoclastic act itself visible; total erasure would also erase the iconoclastic gesture and its meaning.[69]

A further strategy of playing with precedents to prompt reflection is showcased by Hans Haake's installation in the Reichstag which reads 'To the Population', an ironic variation of the official inscription 'To the German People' on the front of the building. The latter had been designed by the influential architect Peter Behrens (Mies van der Rohe and Walter Gropius apprenticed in his office). It had been cast from two cannons surrendered in Prussia's wars against Napoleon and mounted in 1916; it constituted both a characteristically awkward attempt by Wilhem II to gain popularity, and a quite accurate expression of how the Kaiser viewed the political system: it was his choice to hand his *Volk* a parliament: a gracious gift, *von Kaisers Gnaden*. Haake not only reminds the people that the word *Volk* can no longer be used innocently in Germany; he also prompts reflection on the not exactly uncontaminated notion of *Boden* (as in *Blut und Boden*): deputies are invited to bring soil from their constituencies to fill the space around the neon 'Der Bevölkerung' sign; there is now a wild garden, which anyone can 'access' through a webcam documenting the uncontrolled growth of greenery from across the country.[70] True, only some historical background knowledge makes this monument meaningful. But is that an argument against it? After all, democratic states do have means of providing their populations with relevant knowledge; in fact, it is imperative – starting with civic education in schools – that they do so.

Ironic, or clearly subversive, variations on previous iconographic programmes may well spark conflicts; but, as I have been stressing throughout, conflicts are normal and ideally productive in a democracy; they are certainly preferable to the outcome that Robert Musil famously remarked on when he observed that monuments are the most invisible things in the world: they become part of the landscape.[71] This prompted him, in what was, after all, a satirical piece, to argue that it was clearly malicious to devote a monument to someone – it constituted the surest way to consign them to oblivion. Continuing in a satirical vein, he demanded that monuments – 'like all of us' – should make more of an effort and fulfil what Musil identified as a monument's core function: some kind of PR. So, rather than just having a statue of Goethe, Musil recommended installing a huge sign screaming 'Goethe is the best!'

There is no reason for democracies to stay away from the monumental as such; there's also no reason to stay away from monuments (after all, the statues we discussed earlier screamed 'Harmodios and Aristogeiton were the best!') – but, in the end, the creation of what have been called counter-monuments and anti-monuments is most fitting.[72] A counter-monument is juxtaposed to an existing one rightly perceived as problematic.[73] An example is the Austrian sculptor Alfred Hrdlicka's structure right next to a Nazi monument devoted to soldiers in Hamburg: the original, erected in 1936, glorifies a homogeneous group of men shouldering rifles. Hrdlicka's complex construction cannot be grasped immediately; on closer inspection it reveals itself as showing scenes of destruction, with humans burning and drowning.

By contrast, an anti-monument does not so much counter another monument as question monumentality as such; it seeks to sensitize citizens to damage, loss, the fragmented, or the unfinished.[74] Counter-monuments stage a conflict, rather than suggest veneration; anti-monuments also challenge spectators and sometimes even prompt a form of participation: after all, democracy's promise is not just collective freedom; it is also individual autonomy.[75] A monument that tells you what to think seems prima facie not to live up to that promise; an anti-monument that tells you what to think about – and then allows for expression of that thinking process – seems much more likely to fulfil that democratic promise. Jochen Gerz's Monument Against Fascism invited people to write on a stele displayed in the working-class district of Hamburg-Harburg. The structure not only invited its own vandalization; it also slowly disappeared into the ground, the opposite of an ambition for immortality (with, if we are to believe Musil, resulting invisibility).[76]

Or consider the Gramsci Monument, a temporary creation by the Swiss artist Thomas Hirschhorn in a housing project in the Bronx in New York. It was erected by local residents and featured a bar, a stage, as well as a library, all adorned with sentences from Gramsci's *Prison Notebooks*. One can condemn such an endeavour as political kitsch and lament art becoming an 'event' promising all-too-easy participation (have a drink at the bar!); one can question whether it remotely lived up to the kinds of political strategies that the Italian Marxist himself had called for – remake culture; remake what people consider common sense; start a process of continuous education. But there was something about its experimental nature that at least held out the promise of activating underprivileged people as democratic citizens. The German artist Frieder Schnock once observed, 'A memorial has to say, "You are someone. You have someone else in front of you right now. You will not be alone." '[77] Gerz sounded a similar note when he claimed: 'People, not monuments, are the places of memory.' We don't know of course – and I admit this might be a bit of a stretch – but even the seemingly straightforwardly heroic Tyrannicides in Athens might have forced citizens to do some thinking for themselves, if they were aware of the complicated story around private love and public democratic action.

Can an invitation to interaction be combined with an encouragement to engage democracy's pluralism? Consider Bjarke Ingels' *Superkilen* ('Superwedge') in Copenhagen, where items from many different countries are on display in a park at the centre of an ethnically diverse neighbourhood, Nørrebro. Again, some might conclude immediately: multiculturalism kitsch. According to an ethnographer, the 108 objects drawn from a multitude of cultural contexts, from swings to lamps, only represent diversity; they do not really

encourage interaction with the objects, or, even more important, among people with differing backgrounds.[78] Defenders
of the project argue that the artistic group that selected the
objects, Superflex, actually worked closely with people living
in the area; in fact, they even took groups of locals to specific
countries to choose something to bring to Copenhagen.[79]
Some objects are for actual everyday use – and apparently
are used every day: kids play in the fountain, young men
train in the boxing ring, families have barbeques, people sit
on the benches. The daughter of a friend of mine who had
to pass through the area on the way to school remarked that
the big neon sign from Rochester, PA, that said 'Delightfully
Different Donuts' was always a source of disappointment –
because no doughnut shop ever opened.[80] Maybe not objects
that prompt exercises in democratic autonomy – but also not
the invisibility of which Musil warned.

'Make it look more democratic, Mikhail Mikhailovich!'

It is time to move inside buildings. What really matters beyond
the more or less empty square on the outside is having inside
spaces that facilitate a range of democratic practices. Such
spaces can suggest different political dramaturgies through
different shapes and sequencing of spaces; they can also cue
people through variations in iconography and atmosphere.[81]
Once more, it would be wrong to assume something like 'the
more open, the more democratic' or 'the more transparent,
the more democratic'. Above all, it would be wrong to assume
that democracy is reducible to a single activity.

'Debating chambers' is often used as shorthand for parliaments. But that is a misunderstanding, consciously encouraged by critics of parliamentarism: the arch-antiliberal legal theorist Carl Schmitt held that the original ideal of parliament – with the word derived from *parlare* – relied on the notion that 'truth' or at least rational policies would emerge from free and open discussion.[82] There are indeed moments when speakers challenge each other with arguments in front of packed parliaments, the UK's Prime Minister's Question Time being an obvious example. The value of the confrontation is not that people inside parliament will change their minds; it is that disagreement is dramatized such that citizens comprehend the distinct views of government and opposition. Yet these are exceptional moments; and only in authoritarian states are assemblies always filled with attentively listening deputies who, we can safely assume, are also perfectly compliant politically.[83]

The notion of legislatures as providing a stage for what Schmitt derided as a *clasa discutadora* misses an important element of actual, working parliaments:[84] parliamentary procedures are not designed primarily to enable an endless, freewheeling exchange of views; rather, they aim at reaching collectively binding decisions: even the longest American filibuster can eventually be brought to an end. What is staged as a debate seldom holds much surprise: the very fact that an issue comes to the floor often means that it has already been decided in backroom negotiations. That does not make the debate meaningless; it just has a different meaning than the one that an anti-parliamentarian like Schmitt ascribed to it.

Much of the real work of parliaments happens in committees, sometimes visible, sometimes not so visible. German deputies are fond of describing the Paul-Löbe-Haus, with its large cylinder-like forms on the outside, as 'the engine room of democracy', since most committees meet there.[85] Here the naive endorsement of total transparency is particularly unhelpful. Whereas debates can serve to dramatize differences, committees do the slow, hard work of accountability; the latter hardly ever take the form of a 'gotcha' question in front of rolling cameras. In Germany, most inquiries – de facto criticisms – initiated by the opposition are in any case answered in writing.[86] It is in fact in committees that an opposition can have real influence; for that, the public dramatization of conflict is sometimes precisely to be avoided.

Any suggestion that there could be an 'ideal form' of parliaments – be it oblong benches à la Westminster or the semi-circle, sometimes said to facilitate consensus – is implausible, even if politicians sometimes like to pretend otherwise: the speaker of the Duma once instructed the architect charged with creating a new chamber to 'Make it look more democratic, Mikhail Mikhailovich!' by employing a forum-like structure.[87]

Yet the choice is not arbitrary either, because different understandings of what democracy is primarily about can guide it. Government and opposition confronting each other is a straightforward way of dramatizing conflict; it also underlines the notion – far from obvious to anyone until the middle of the nineteenth century – that the opposition is legitimate and functions as a 'government-in-waiting'. The House of Commons is far too small to accommodate all MPs on its benches simultaneously: only 437 out of the 650 representatives can actually sit down; this creates the sense of crowds and urgency that Churchill deemed essential for the adversarial understanding of democracy practised in Britain.[88] As he put it, 'the whole character of the British parliamentary institution depends upon the fact that the House of Commons is an oblong and not a semi-circular structure' – a fact, one has to add, that resulted from the former use of the space for choir stalls, not from some theorist designing the ideal room for a two-party democratic system. Churchill also insisted that 'a small chamber and a sense of intimacy are indispensable'. The fact that British parliamentarians have no fixed place – and no desks at all – strengthens the sense that parties are there to oppose each other in words, not to work, whether individually or collectively, on policy details (but also not to bang on tables); the fact that members address the Speaker, and cannot always see colleagues to their side, might suggest this: one's own side needs no persuading.[89]

The American Senate has long ceased to be the world's 'greatest deliberative body', a view attributed to President James Buchanan (himself one of the most spectacular failures in office). In fact, it is doubtful that this description ever applied outside a few decades in the twentieth century: in the nineteenth, an anti-slavery senator from Massachusetts was attacked on the floor by a South Carolina Congressman with a cane (the latter survived a censure resolution in the House and was duly re-elected).

To be sure, configuration and equipment of the Senate make it clear why, in principle, 'deliberative body' is not absurd. Jefferson's 'natural aristocracy' was to convene in a calm atmosphere, with each senator working studiously at his desk, not immediately subject to partisan 'crowd' behaviour, and ideally free from 'urgency' which might lead to rash decisions. Half-circles make for inter-visibility, as on the *Pnyx* and subsequently in the Theatre of Dionysus. If partisan lines are not already clear, and if outcomes aren't already decided before being debated on the floor, it might really matter that one can catch cues about the reactions of allies and adversaries.

The one form that finds least support in any plausible theory of democracy is the 'classroom model': the teachers have elevated positions at the front, everyone else sits in rows facing them. The Duma looks like this (Mikhail Mikhailovich did not succeed in 'making it look more democratic'), as does the 'parliament' in Beijing. Konrad Adenauer would have preferred this configuration, dating back to the Bismarck era, with the government visibly elevated above deputies. It is easy to read such a design as authoritarian, but one might also understand this kind of direct confrontation, in systems where government and parliament are entirely separated, as an awkward attempt to suggest accountability – except that the image of all rows dutifully filled with deputies has precisely become an emblem of authoritarianism, not of anything like a particularly strong check on executive power.

If parliamentarism is understood less as facilitating the exchange of views among representatives with equal claims to legitimacy and more as a device to force power-holders to provide answers, a crucial question becomes where and how the power-holders are located. In one sense, Adenauer's wish came true: in the Reichstag, the government sits above the deputies and can only be addressed by someone facing the plenary if they turn slightly away from most deputies, their presumed main audience. In Israel, ministers are at the same level as the other members of the Knesset, sitting around a table – but they turn their backs to them. In France, the first row of the Assemblée Nationale is reserved for members of the government; a very visible speaker can address them from the podium – literally talk down to them – but their reactions will remain invisible to most *députés*. A configuration that ensures direct address *and* can make for a meaningful back-and-forth – while also signalling that politicians are ultimately on an equal footing – can be found in Italy's Montecitorio (a baroque papal palace, and the oldest building housing a democratic assembly): here ministers sit at a table facing the deputies, on the same level, purposefully vulnerable to questioning and criticism.[90] At the same time, there is little vulnerability to questioning and criticism from citizens, as the latter have no space to gather outside the palazzo originally designed by Bernini (and they are allowed to visit the place of their representatives only once per month).

Configurations of space can reveal a shared understanding of what democracy is primarily for – again, think of the notion that the people ought to have a clear choice between government and opposition. But sometimes it is not the greatest promise of the political system, but what was perceived as the greatest threat to it which appears to have determined the shape of a decision-making body. A not so well-known, but telling, example of a space that still exists but without the crucial interior design is the Grand Council in the Doge's Palace. Venice was hardly a democracy; it boasted what admirers considered a mixed constitution, with the Doge as a quasi-monarch (albeit an elected one), a Senate, and the Grand Council (which, however, hardly meant 'the people' – membership was inherited by aristocratic families). In the *Maggior Consiglio* up to 2,000 men sat on long wooden benches running the length of the room;

they faced each other, rather than the Doge and his counsellors who sat at the head of the enormous room, in front of a Tintoretto painting, *Il Paradiso*, that to this day remains the largest oil painting in the world (22 x 9 metres).

The members usually cast ballots in silence (again, perhaps, Rousseau's republican intuition: don't talk, just look within and concentrate on the common good).[91] The fear was of corruption – and the configuration of the space made for perfect surveillance (or, put more neutrally, inter-visibility, the notion we already encountered in ancient Athens): aristocrats watched each other, side conversations were difficult, and, in any case, whatever they said could also be heard by someone behind them; for good measure, there were benches on the sides of the *sala* where additional observers were seated.[92] But, on a more positive note, the configuration also sent a message about the equality of the members: there was no 'front bench', no designated leaders of factions; there were only peers intently reflecting on the *bene comune*.

Different ways of arranging space, then, teach participants in politics different things, subtly or not so subtly; they suggest different dramaturgies and create different atmospheres. One of the most vexing political challenges of the past few years is which stance politicians should adopt vis-à-vis far-right populists; after all, they have appeared in parliaments in Sweden and Spain for the first time. Should they be excluded entirely – from coalitions for sure, but perhaps also from any cooperation in committee work, even from political conversation *tout court*? Or ought one to have some hope for strategies of 'moderation through inclusion'? According to such strategies, once they are made responsible for addressing real problems, extremists of various sorts will have to stop spending all their time grandstanding – and hatemongering – and start to deal pragmatically with actual policy questions, and thereby become more moderate.

These dilemmas will not be solved by architects. But it's not an entirely trivial footnote to the debates about far-right populism that different spaces might facilitate different strategies of relating to what are sometimes euphemistically called 'parliamentary newcomers'. Some spaces are so small and create such intimacy (just as Churchill wished) that one might be forced to engage one another – the corridors in the House of Commons are often lauded as such a site; others are so large that the far right can stick with its tactics of shunning others, as in: 'We shun "the mainstream" before "the mainstream" can shun us.' Self-isolation then facilitates self-radicalization.

Self-radicalization, social scientists tell us with an unusual degree of confidence, is more likely to happen in homogeneous groups. As we already saw, it is not true that something known as 'the internet' necessarily creates 'filter bubbles' and 'echo chambers'. This facile, though also oddly comforting, technological determinism ('everything's awful, but at least I know why it's happening!') has repeated a long-established pattern of blaming political pathologies on media innovations: the printing press caused the wars of religion; radio gave us Hitler; TV made Joseph McCarthy inevitable. But the diagnosis fails to distinguish between 'the internet' and the business model of particular platforms, some of which can indeed be described as 'incitement capitalism', based on the monetization of outrage and anger.[93]

While we need to resist entering an echo chamber about echo chambers – faithfully confirming to each other that filter bubbles are causing all our political misery – we also do need to understand how parliaments today function differently on the basis of new technological possibilities: some deputies spend more time curating their image online than engaging colleagues in the supposed halls of power; what happens in the plenary is no longer aimed either at anyone physically present or at an imagined general public; rather, it is designed to produce instant material for social media, in turn aimed at fundraising among the already committed. Churchill was concerned about the House of Commons being invaded by 'the mass and the machine' – and by machine he meant cameras. In one of his most important observations on how changing media were transforming politics in the 1930s, Walter Benjamin claimed that the then crisis of democracy should be understood as a crisis of the 'capacity to exhibit' – *Ausstellbarkeit* – political human beings; film in particular, he suggested, led to theatres and parliaments being deserted, as the stage actor was being replaced with the movie star, and the great parliamentary debater with the dictator.

Today, it is very simple instantly to represent, and even easier to misrepresent the dramaturgies unfolding in legislatures; think of Senator Ted Cruz, during an important committee hearing, immediately searching for himself on Twitter, after a particularly outrageous set of statements. Unlike with Trump's props – which followed the logic of TV shows – online snippets can pass for conclusive proof, if edited cleverly: they really show the relevant details, unlike Trump's cartoonish piles of paper – but the details can still be framed in a profoundly misleading way.

'Whose House? Our House!'

Having roamed around debating chambers and committee rooms, it's time to turn towards the exterior again, or, rather, to consider transitions between inside and outside. We already saw that getting close to legislatures has both practical and symbolic significance. We also saw that the story of modern political life cannot be told as a simple, linear one of ever more open access. The Renaissance theorist Leon Battista Alberti insisted that only the tyrant had to hole up in a fortress; the legitimate king could be accessible. As he put it, 'a royal palace should be sited in the city centre, should be of easy access, and should be gracefully decorated, elegant and refined'; by contrast, 'that of a tyrant, being a fortress rather than a house, should be positioned where it is neither inside nor outside the city'; it should also, he specified furthermore, 'be set well back on all sides from any buildings'.[94] Congress, as we saw, did not always believe in easy access.

Napoleon held court in the Tuileries but carefully controlled who could get close. Versailles had actually been surprisingly open; it was simply assumed that nobody would just wander into the grounds, let alone the palace.[95] The constraints on access were not exercised by the architecture; instead, rituals and personnel at hand in the palace would have cued people and, if necessary, enforced the rules. A similar pattern can still be observed at today's constitutional court in Karlsruhe: people can get very close to the edifice, there are no fences – but plenty of police will rush in if someone acts suspiciously.[96]

In a democracy, gestures towards common and easy

access – such as an entrance shared by politicians and citizens, as in Canberra – may well trigger the dynamic we observed in the discussion of transparency: deputies will find new paths to exit and enter in order to shield themselves from the gaze (and speech, and possibly touch) of the people. This is precisely what happened in Canberra: spaces designed for staff – so called 'rat runs', accessible only with swipe cards – came to be used by politicians, as these spaces effectively sheltered them from unpredictable encounters with citizens.[97] And when cameras were introduced to make the meetings of the EU Council of Ministers 'more transparent', the real discussions began to take place over lunch – when no one was listening.[98]

At least on a symbolic level, some gestures towards access and inclusion are more plausible than others. Robespierre wanted 12,000 citizens on the galleries of the National Assembly (his wish was never fulfilled). Inside today's Reichstag plenary, the galleries are larger than in the House of Commons and intrude into the elliptical space. Here citizens watching and listening are also elevated above their representatives, but they are harder to ignore than the shadows in the dome above (of course, people have to behave themselves; even holding a mobile phone is not permitted).

Across from the Reichstag, the Löbe building features a ground floor that resembles a street (and continues what should have been the civic forum on the outside). The street as a site of democratic contestation and citizens acting in concert is symbolically brought into the official house of the deputies; it serves as a reminder that street politics has democratic meaning. A similar pattern can be found in the Maltese parliament designed by Renzo Piano; a largely empty square in Valletta appears to continue into the recessed ground floor of the building (sheathed – you will have guessed it – in glass). The set-up gestures at something like a continuous confrontation between pedestrians and politicians – even if, as usual with glass, it is of course only a gesture.[99]

Do deputies really need all these reminders? In representative democracies with regular elections, politicians are presumably very much aware that the people are breathing down their necks; that is, after all, what distinguishes our systems from the Athenian one, but also the Roman, in which, as we saw, elites were regularly talking at the people, in *contiones*, but were not truly accountable to them. So perhaps the citizens are the real addressees: the buildings are supposed to teach them something, not the representatives.

What might they teach the representatives beyond the rather obvious need for accountability? Architects of parliaments have tried to provide a range of cues beyond invoking the presence of the people; some are meant to signal very specific expectations of how an elected representative is to behave. The architect Günter Behnisch left the concrete surface outside the entrance of Bonn's new parliament – which replaced the edifice that allegedly lacked 'splendour' – rough and uneven; this was intended as a reminder of democracy's pluralism (one is left to wonder whether the smooth wooden floor on the inside signalled that there'd be consensus in the end); he also made the stairs leading down to the chamber so steep that one had to concentrate hard in order not to fall – a cue that deputies should really be present and make an effort, or just a thoughtless imposition on the infirm? Louis Kahn would have said: the former; for his ambition had also been to cue politicians for the special nature of assembly: according to Kahn, 'an assembly is a transcendent place. A place, no matter what kind of a rogue you are, when you go into an assembly somehow you may vote for the right thing.'[100]

Enric Miralles, architect of the Scottish Parliament, built special bay windows from stainless steel and framed in oak; inside they featured shelving and a leather seat – potentially putting a politician on display to the outside world. Miralles had intended them as 'contemplation spaces' – suggesting that MSPs should behave, at least occasionally, like monks, or like Rousseau's ideal citizens, introspecting in thinking pods in order to discern the common good.[101] He also wanted to remind them of the presence of the people when legislating: the wall of the chamber facing the 127 MSPs features silhouettes of citizens (which the innocent observer – meaning, me, on my first visit – might mistake for stylized images of whisky bottles); the LED lights above the Members also

Scottish parliament: Where parliamentarians are supposed to think long and hard.

show 127 miniature figures. Really a reminder that the people are watching – or, in fact, visual confirmation that the people are only ever a ghostly presence at best?

Gestures 'to bring the people in' are easy to ridicule, or at least to condemn as hypocritical. For instance, with ever-tighter security it can seem that the internal street or square only adds insult to civic injury: after all, in the case of Berlin, it isn't really a street, and it's extending a forum that was vetoed by Kohl and all subsequent German chancellors. What still merits consideration though – quite apart from the bureaucratic obstacles to overcome before entering galleries or meeting one's deputy in their office – is how individuals might *experience* a way in, comparable perhaps to the manner the Gothic cathedral, unlike Speer's architecture, was meant to remain accessible despite its awe-inspiring size. Especially in large, diverse (and possibly federal) states, one way is to enable citizens to connect what might prima facie be an intimidating structure with the more local worlds with which they are familiar. The representation of the individual states in the Congress building's Hall of the People is an attempt to provide such connections; Lutyens' allusions to India's diversity in his government architecture was another (an aspect that disappeared with the new parliament constructed under Modi).[102]

Of course, all such talk of giving citizens a sense of the legislature as a 'palace of the people' and 'allowing them a way in' sounds different after 2021. 'This is our house!' the American insurrectionists kept yelling on 6 January about the Capitol; similar rhetoric had been heard among those trying to 'take' the Reichstag in August 2020. Rather than seeing Congress's Hall of the People as a representation of their different federal identities, the Trump storm troops literally shat in – and possibly on – it.

The issue is not the desirability, let alone the permissibility, of large demonstrations in front of legislatures; it's also not whether citizens should or shouldn't try to get under the skin of professional politicians (of course they should be able to try that). What was particular – and in need of explanation – about 6 January 2021 was that those who declared themselves 'the real people', and who had been addressed as such by Trump in his speech at the Ellipse, did not just occupy their house, but also vandalized it.

A key is found when examining more closely a phenomenon that characterizes far-right parties and movements in very different countries: to put it bluntly, the promise to restore entitlements to white men who think that women, nature, as well as the machinery of democracy, including the buildings which house that machinery, are ultimately something like their *personal property*.

Not enough thought has been given to the basic fact that the Capitol was 'taken', and that those who entered it displayed an astonishing sense of entitlement, with 'This is our House!' its most obvious expression. Observers at the time noted that some of the insurrectionists behaved almost like tourists, but tourists generally – and God-fearing conservative ones in particular – know that they are not supposed to just grab, deface, or outright destroy what they see.

To get at the deeper meaning of the events, a concept coined by the German philosopher Eva von Redecker is helpful: 'phantom possession', a term inspired by well-known phenomena such as phantom pain and phantom limbs.[103]

White men used to be entitled to certain things, and even human beings, as their de facto property: the natural environment was just there for the taking; and women were simply expected to provide sex, esteem, care, as well as all kinds of other services, and, not least, let their reproductive capacities be subject to men's control.

True, territory conquered by colonialists was first declared *terra nullius* (even if there had been someone there before), and it could then be bought and sold; by contrast, it was not true, for the most part, that women could be sold like property (whereas men can indeed always buy sexual services).[104] But coverture still meant that women were effectively under the control of men; it is easy to forget that in some Western democracies wives could not accept employment without their husband's consent until the 1970s, while marital rape was not outlawed until the 1990s. As W.E.B. DuBois pointed out, the right to feel superior to, and outright oppress, certain groups compensated poorer whites for some of the domination they suffered themselves; it generated a 'psychological wage' in addition to the monetary one.[105]

One of the hallmarks of modern property is that you can do with it more or less what you want. That includes the right to destroy it. The British jurist William Blackstone famously described property as 'that sole and despotic dominion which one man claims and exercises over the external things of the world'; the Napoleonic Code included a right to abuse and even destroy property. This legal dimension is one thing; the psychological one another: it can seem that destruction proves that something is really mine; after all, I can do with it whatever I want, no matter how abusive. That disastrous dynamic becomes visible when men try to kill women they claim to love, rather than put up with emancipation – which literally means the exit from property, or *mancipium*.

It might not come as a surprise, then, that the vast number of the insurrectionists at the Capitol were men, with many displaying military gear. The man who put his feet up on a desk in the office of Nancy Pelosi, Speaker of the House of Representatives, from which he also stole mail, no doubt tried to assert 'despotic dominion'. Destruction promises to make the phantom real – and perhaps make the pain go away.

Explaining to far-right fanatics what democracy is really about, or that they are in fact destroying the thing they claim to value, can be beside the point, if their underlying assumption remains: if it's not exactly as I want it, I'd rather destroy it, including what is supposed to be 'my House'; and for sure no one else – and especially not majorities consisting of black and brown people – can have it.

The attack on the Capitol created a script – a dramaturgy, if you like – easily copied elsewhere. Supporters of the Brazilian president Jair Bolsonaro enacted it on 8 January 2023. The background was by now mind-numbingly familiar: an incumbent crying fraud even before the voting had started, declaring victory in the face of an outcome not to his liking (different was the role of the military, creating fears of a coup backed by soldiers, not just Bolsonaro fans in soccer shirts). The insurrectionists in Brazil were even more brutal than the MAGA crowd in their attack on what was supposedly their house in Washington, DC. Not only was glass broken by Brazilian protestors; not only did they vandalize interior spaces; artworks commissioned by Oscar Niemeyer were destroyed.[106] It's possible to read what happened as an aggression against modernism (and a Communist architect!); but we still know too little about what in particular was supposed to have been annihilated in the insurrection.[107]

Wrapped in Ruins

After 6 January 2021 the Capitol, from the outside, looked pretty much as always; the government buildings in Brasília, on the other hand, were obviously damaged. In light of these attacks, there is something eerie about one of Louis Kahn's architectural ideas: he often talked about 'wrapping ruins' around his buildings. The sense of the fragmentary that came with many of Kahn's edifices did not so much suggest future decay, though; rather, it could be read as a sign of things not really being finished. Kahn wanted to make the construction process visible, allowing people to experience a monumental, seemingly unfinished building as what he called an 'offering' to architecture.

A building designed for complex, often precisely timed political processes cannot be literally unfinished. But it can be modular and easily extendable: Axel Schultes and Charlotte Frank's Federal Ribbon in Berlin has been extended already; their Chancellery is also set to be enlarged. Less tangibly, it can convey a sense of Michelangelo's *non finito* – something that, symbolically, aligns with democracy's self-conception as an ongoing, open process.[108] Of course, a building simply ends up lying, if what goes on inside does not align at all with such allusions to openness and indeterminacy. The great eighteenth-century architect Étienne-Louis Boullée's demand for poetic sentiments analogous to specific functions can be translated into the notion – by now familiar – that buildings cue us in the right ways. But parliaments should not become emotion-producing machines: the evocation of a function is not enough. At the risk of stating the obvious: the building actually has to function in the right ways.

While conveying a sense of the unfinished, Kahn's parliament building in Dhaka also impresses onlookers as something else: it can seem like a fortress.[109] The people had indeed been pushed further and further away from the Jatiya Sangsad Bhaban: the South Plaza had been closed in 2005; a fence was erected around the whole Capitol Complex in 2015 (putting an end to families picnicking and celebrating on the green spaces around the parliament – a space that had been especially valued in one of the most densely populated cities in the world).

Ceaușescu's grotesque palace in Bucharest had always featured a wall around the huge complex, three kilometres long in total; efforts by civic groups and architects to have it

Brasília: A man walks atop Oscar Niemeyer's modernist masterpiece. In 2013, protestors occupied the roof; in 2023, supporters of former president Jair Bolsonaro stormed and damaged the buildings.

removed – something that would hardly have endangered politicians – have been successfully resisted by the Romanian political elite. We get back to the point made earlier: a state can send a message about people being in principle welcome; or it can send a message about people in principle being distrusted. In retrospect, there is something peculiar about Joe Biden calling the Capitol a 'citadel of democracy' in his 2022 State of the Union address.

The Other Palaces of the People

The 'stormings' of 2020, 2021, 2023, and 2024 in Berlin, Washington, DC, Brasília, and Dhaka do not invalidate the arguments for a democratic 'siege' made in the previous chapter. But they do force us anew to consider, beyond large demonstrations, delegations visiting deputies, or school classes being dutifully shepherded through parliaments on an annual civic excursion, how best to 'bring the people' close – or even in.

One answer would point to edifices discussed earlier: the politics-cum-culture palaces in state socialist countries. Recall that the Greek agora had multiple uses and purposes; it was after the Roman conquest that a political agora – by then the site of an imperial cult, not anything remotely democratic – was clearly separated from one devoted to market exchange. Also recall that Aristotle had objected to the multi-use model all along. One sensible worry is this: the fact that bowling happened next to the Volkskammer in the East German Palace of the Republic precisely demonstrated that the parliament was in the end as unpolitical (and, in the grand scheme of things, as unimportant) as the bowling.

The dignity of legislation needs to be communicated clearly to citizens.[110] One of the (many, many) problems with Trump's privatization of government work at Mar-a-Lago is that it turned politics into a consumerist spectacle; another was that the rules of access could no longer be traced back to a process of democratic decision-making; instead, they conformed to the logic of a private club driven by the profit-motive, including profiting from showing off government documents that were not supposed to have been there in the first place.[111]

There's a strong argument for separation, but the argument does not apply equally to palace and square: in the former, multiple uses end up denigrating the political, and, in any case, the point is not to bring in as many citizens as possible; with the latter, offering only a political function means that the square is unlikely to fulfil its overall democratic purpose. It needs to attract people, and, as the urban theorist Holly Whyte observed, people attract people. They have all kinds of reasons to be in the square, and politics may well be an incidental by-product. The square being a place of entertainment, or good for commerce, does not take away from the dignity of politics.[112]

Separation of the location for collectively binding decisions should ideally go together with properly financing the kinds of spaces state socialists lauded as 'social condensers'. Sociologists have rightly emphasized the importance of 'third spaces' – not private homes, not workplaces – for people to meet and engage in cooperation, often not directly political at all. These might create stronger bonds and possible bridges to groups one does not regularly encounter – though, again, these outcomes will be incidental.[113] The public library remains the prime example of such a space; another is the swimming pool, at least the municipal and not the fancy private one. As Josiah Stamp, one-time director of the Bank of England, observed in 1936: 'Bathing reduces rich and poor, high and low, to a common standard of enjoyment and health. When we get down to swimming, we get down to democracy' (never mind that attire – as well as body shape – can communicate all kinds of status differences).[114]

So, what might we say in the end about the design of, in Kahn's words, 'legislative palaces'? They should signal that something important happens in them – collectively binding decisions are made here, decisions that will eventually authorize the state's coercion of those who resist them. The buildings should dignify, but not glorify; they should be serious, but not severe ('severity' is one truly common denominator of fascist architecture – no such thing as irony or playfulness in Fascism).

The inside spaces of legislatures have to accommodate a formalized sequencing of political events, as opposed to the simultaneous, much more chaotic politics that unfolds on squares and streets. In that sense even the most democratic legislatures will always have a whiff of the royal palace, with its rituals and control by courtiers and servants. One does not have to go as far as Jean Genet. The French writer, in an extraordinary passage, remarked apropos palaces, that, in one sense, they were the same as prisons: he observed that 'the rigour of the rules, their strictness, their precision are in essence the same as the etiquette of a royal court, as the exquisite and tyrannical politeness of which a guest at that court is the object'.[115]

Legislatures must indeed have 'rigour', 'rules', 'precision' – often enforced by uniformed personnel who would not be out of place in a royal palace; these orient citizens properly. One of the – many – disturbing things about Ceaușescu's palace is that it has no clear hierarchy of rooms. Versailles is like an eel trap – one simply had to keep moving towards the king; in Bucharest one wanders from one large space, over-decorated and usually featuring enormous chandeliers, to another. The effect is overwhelming and at the same time entirely disorienting.[116] To be sure, had the palace ever been used by Ceaușescu and his wife (who at the time were informally known as no. 1 and no. 2), plenty of people would have been present to direct individuals to specific locations and reinforce particular routes through the edifice. But the logic of the spaces simply was different from Versailles, including the fact that no. 1 and no. 2 had their designated offices at the side of the building – supposedly to make an escape easier, in case things were not going according to plan. In Versailles, all rooms led to the king; in Bucharest, there had to be an escape route from the people.

Dhaka: Good to have a boat outside parliament. But Kahn's building has become less and less accessible over the years.

What Kahn called a 'society of rooms' needs to offer spaces for the different dramaturgies of democracy. Unlike the palace and the prison, parliament must make space for conflict. True, this risks democracy itself becoming a spectacle, yet another thing to be consumed. Arguments for how to stage debates, deliberations, and negotiations rely on the assumption that it will still be possible to find a proper public for each of them. Architecture can help in orienting such a public; it cannot create it.

How does one connect the rooms in a 'society of rooms'? Kahn's answer was a street on the inside of his parliament. Walking on it, one feels like being in a modern city: looking up at tall concrete walls with occasional openings, one gets glimpses of different rooms – such as the mosque integrated into the building.

What else does the street do that the rooms themselves – and squares – cannot do?

3

Street: Streaming and Blocking

A city should be a place where a little boy walking through its streets can sense what he someday would like to be.

Louis Kahn

The street is disorder.

Henri Lefebvre

To thread one's way through an immense and ever moving crowd is a peculiar and salutary experience. All merged into one great stream, yet each manages to find his way to his own goal. In the midst of so many people and all their commotion, I feel peaceful and alone for the first time. The louder the upper opera of the streets, the quieter I become.

Goethe, *Italian Journey*, Naples (17 March 1787)

In the modern political imagination, the street – much more than the square – has always signified democratic hopes and triggered anxieties about disorder. Streets are unavoidable in the way squares are not; Jane Jacobs wrote in her classic account of city life as it *actually* unfolds, as opposed to what planners might dream about: 'streets and their sidewalks, the main public spaces of a city, are its most vital organs'.[1] Yet

Benjamin's observation that the built environment is perceived by us in a state of distraction applies to streets much more than squares. The latter seek, and usually receive, attention; we might hurry across a square, but still recognize it as something distinctive; squares tend to offer a focal point, be it a monument, a fountain, or, for that matter, a tree, as with the oldest Greek *plateía*, or town square.[2] Streets are no less a matter of design than squares. But, contrary to a cliché of squares being potentially dangerously populist, as a long tradition of anti-democratic thought would have it, the street is usually of much more concern to the authorities: for the street can be harder to control.

This chapter reassesses the meaning of streets for democracy. On one very basic level, better conditions for circulation spell freedom: Voltaire, when visiting London, was deeply impressed with the pavements, which made it easier for those without carriages to get around; pavements, he thought, democratize the city.[3] However, we need to relativize – not outright reject – two further ideas about how streets and democracy are connected, ideas that have become conventional wisdom in our time. According to many street boosters, streets are sites for encountering the demos in its diversity as well as sites for informal community-building, part of a larger democratic way of life. I want to suggest that the first is empirically often implausible in the light of widespread, and perfectly legitimate, norms of 'street conduct'. The second depends on a kind of projection of village life into cities. That is not in and of itself problematic, but it might come with some of the well-known oppressive aspects of community-oriented understandings of politics. Instead of these conventional conceptions of city street life, I'll try to make the case for streets as sites of *privacy in public*, a particular form of anonymity that allows for self-invention and re-invention, promises long and rightly associated with the modern metropolis.

There's something else still: I also want to emphasize the street as a unique site for protest – an affordance that has certainly fed the cliché of streets as sites of irrational crowd behaviour. It is specifically as sites of protest that streets might actually meet expectations of spontaneous encounters with others: for during protests, strangers will be in each other's faces; and they might find it much easier to just connect. Note again that protest is not the same as prefiguration; the former can really use streets; the latter can hardly ever take place on them.

I then discuss two particular threats to democratic street life today. On the one hand, streets increasingly provide access to our selves – that is to say: some of our most intimate information – via ever-proliferating sensors and electronic eyes. This kind of surveillance is bound to have a chilling effect on protest. Second – and we briefly touched on this in the first chapter – democracies are becoming less tolerant of protest as such; new restrictions apply to all kinds of spaces, but to streets in particular.

'Take back the streets' is thus acquiring new political meanings: we need to take streets back *from* surveillance and make them available *for* diverse groups of people to engage in political conduct.

Where the Races Meet?

Precisely because the street is unavoidable, or so it's often claimed, the street must be a space in which the diversity of the demos is most likely to be experienced. The streets, Leonard Cohen sang in his acerbic 'Democracy' from the early 1990s, are the 'holy places where the races meet'. Streets, it is conventionally asserted, enable the unexpected encounter; they allow us to experience difference without fear.[4] A similar logic might hold for certain forms of public transportation or state offices and, in some countries, hospitals – people who do not usually interact find themselves (involuntarily) in the same space. As the social theorist Dilip Parameshwar Gaonkar puts it in a statement that encapsulates much of laudatory political thinking about streets: 'The street is where people mingle; where they size one another up; where *mutual display* occurs; where common horizons, however fleetingly, are established.'[5]

Note how such a view depends on several assumptions: the street needs to be a space not just for fleeting encounters, but for some form of engagement ('mingling'). People must pay at least some attention to each other ('mutual display'). And somehow, from mutual engagement emerges some sense of a shared world ('common horizons'), though of course not necessarily shared world views. One question is whether mingling must involve explicit mutual address; or whether seeing each other – 'mutual display' – is sufficient to have the effects that proponents of a democratic politics of the streets desire. If seeing is enough, how does seeing difference translate into, let's say, acceptance or perhaps even affirmation of diversity? One answer is a variation of the famous 'contact hypothesis': what or who was thought of as threatening before becomes familiar and is revealed as non-threatening.[6] An alternative goes one step further from mere acceptance: here the idea is that diversity in and of itself generates a form of aesthetic pleasure, and that pluralism is perceived as enriching, an effect observable in situations where there were prejudices to start with, but also in ones where citizens were broadly free of preconceived notions. In either case: seeing is simply assumed to be transformative.[7]

It should be fairly obvious that these are contingent outcomes. Seeing someone is evidently not the same as accepting someone; other felicitous conditions have to be in place for one to turn into the other. (This difficulty also haunted the organizers of the revolutionary festivals in France: mutual observation during rituals did not reliably produce the desired patriotic dispositions.) The contexts of the streets themselves matter: obviously, what is perceived as a threatening street environment is not exactly conducive to seeing strangers as non-threatening. Here again, cuing proves crucial. The spatial arrangement itself does not necessarily do this (though it can: think of the stereotypical example of the long dark alley); more likely, it is facades, or what the nineteenth-century architect and theorist Gottfried Semper called the 'clothing' of buildings. 'Clothing' implies that there can be 'ragged' or 'torn' or simply in some sense unattractive clothing. Both the shape of spaces and the scenography of streets matter in setting the stage for encounters; and the stage can be more or less conducive to such encounters having anything like positive civic effects.

So, there is no straightforward psychological mechanism connecting street life and democratic attitudes. The same is true of accounts that view street life as essential for something more ambitious, moving beyond attitudes to conduct: the idea of streets as a privileged site for community-building. The notion that one gets familiar with others plays a role here, too, but so does the expectation that proximity will lead one to identify common problems, usually by falling into casual conversation.

As we saw, the idea of the democratic city as one of incessant chatter goes as far back as Plato – and Plato found fault with that very characteristic; more recently, the American philosopher John Dewey advanced the notion that neighbourhoods with people used to talking are primary units for democratic community-building. He claimed that 'there is no substitute for the vitality and depth of close and direct intercourse and attachment . . . Democracy begins at home, and its home is the neighborly community.'[8] Community is impossible without communication, and the street is a space in which informal communication, from rumours to common complaints, happen without barriers that might put citizens off – barriers often associated with official sites of decision-making: complicated meeting rules; a formal atmosphere; the need confidently to speak to large audiences; sometimes the requirement to employ legally precise language.

From this perspective, lingering and loitering – which prima facie serve no purpose – are in fact supremely useful politically. What Jacobs lauded as 'little public sidewalk contacts' help increase trust but also aid in casual opinion-formation on matters of common concern.[9] From minimal levels of trust, so this line of reasoning further suggests, can follow coordinated political activity, for trust means that people one does not know terribly well can be assumed to be of good will and at least somewhat competent to do what they say they will do. Simply helping each other out, or just repeatedly providing basic information, and trusting one another as a result – these are undemanding ways to weave what Jacobs called 'a public web of respect and trust' and to increase the potential for more ambitious forms of political action in the future.[10]

Not all of this will literally be happening on the street: focal points like attractive stoops, or the corner shop, or an institution like the traditional Greek *kafenio* or the Turkish *kahvehane* (which are inside spaces), or the 'third places' we discussed briefly in the previous chapter, might be the most likely contenders.[11] It matters that such places are ones where different people are, so to speak, streaming through; they are public and fluid, but they also contain spaces for relative privacy – allowing individuals to decide for themselves how much they seek to engage others and possibly reveal information about themselves. They also offer possibilities simply to retreat into broadly non-communicative behaviour without seeming odd. Unlike the workplace or, let's say, supermarkets, these other focal points do not have clearly designated singular functions, they are 'open-minded' (to pick up Michael Walzer's terms again, rather than 'single-minded'), with wide latitude for conduct, in the way, let's say, the welfare office is not. They do not cue uniquely applicable norms of behaviour, unless, as in traditional Greek and Turkish coffee houses, they are heavily gendered spaces – not a trivial aspect at all, of course, but also not inevitable.

However, note how a number of preconditions need to be present for such democratic visions to become remotely plausible: people must perceive themselves as members of the same relevant group; they must feel comfortable enough to talk to strangers in the first place; and they must have at least minimum confidence in their own political efficacy: as is well-known from accounts like those of Saul Alinsky, the father of community organizing in the United States, the first two conditions might not be that difficult to meet; but fulfilling the third does not necessarily follow and can be very, very hard to generate – hence the need for community organizers like Alinsky in the first place.[12] Talk can reinforce collective resignation as easily as motivate collective action.

Note also how the first condition – the sense that one shares a certain political space and therefore, in principle, has standing, or, for that matter, might have good reasons to work together towards shared goals – is related to the argument for the moral benefits of exposing oneself to street life; it is assumed that *going out* makes it more likely that one eventually *comes out* in favour of some form of collective action with people one has only seen infrequently but eventually perceives as part of a shared world.

One justification for street festivals and 'block parties' is that they facilitate both the initial positive experience of difference and the willingness to engage in community action. The logic goes back yet again to Rousseau's ideas about the political effects of festivals. Here the 'mutual display' of commitment or even enthusiasm really does seem the right concept, one that can also apply to sports events, concerts, and other occasions where an audience turns into an actor and ends up celebrating itself: people become ever more enthusiastic about their own enthusiasm.

As kitschy as it sounds: festivals can increase actual familiarity; by contrast, rituals and ceremonies create at best a sense of belonging without getting to know anyone. The street might end up providing a non-private and yet intimate sense of being at home in the world with others. This is one reason Benjamin called the street the apartment of the collective and 'the furnished *interieur* of the masses':[13] everyday objects might be repurposed as street furniture; advertisements become what oil paintings are for the bourgeoisie in their homes; walls with the notice *Defense d'Affiche* turn into a writing desk for the people who resolutely ignore the prohibition to write on the walls; and, for those lacking real estate, the café table is like the corner window from which the property owner looks out over their house. Such 'living arrangements' can be created quite easily: people put sofas on the streets and offer free libraries; graffiti becomes a focal point for encounters and a starting point for conversations. The street is no longer what the Futurists derided as a 'doormat'; it wants to be, and becomes, according to Kahn, a room or even a building, and what in a letter to Holly Whyte he called 'a spirit of home beyond one's own'.[14] The artist Pipilotti Rist and the architect Carlos Martinez designed a *Stadtlounge* in the Swiss city of St Gallen; a red carpet, made out of plastic granulate, covers not just the ground but benches and seats; lights that look like boulders hover above what is literally a Red Square in a fairly conservative urban environment.[15] The space is an invitation to make oneself at home; but even those refusing the invitation will be forced to react in one way or another (jolting them out of the default state of distraction that Benjamin diagnosed).

The traditional benefits of casually inhabited outdoor spaces have been recognized by those who sought to replicate street life in very different modern contexts: in post-war Britain, architects and urban designers, increasingly aware of the dire social consequences of modernist tower blocks isolated from street life, advocated 'streets-in-the-sky' and 'deck access' to individual housing units.[16] It had become painfully evident that 'slum clearance' had spelled the loss of something important: architects and urbanists alert to that loss cited all the right arguments ranging from familiarity to security, and, especially, community – the praise of the streets that Jacobs spread so effectively. Peter and Alison Smithson, chief protagonists of British Brutalism, saw streets in the sky as a way to get the best of both worlds: on the one hand, the benefits of clean and efficient social housing (or, in British parlance, 'council housing') that would help reform what the Smithsons called 'moron-made cities';[17] on the other hand, the traditional advantages of the dense working-class neigh-bourhoods that the creations of modernist architects were ruthlessly destroying in the name of 'urban renewal'.[18] They wanted, as Alison Smithson put it, 'systems of linked building complexes . . . intended to correspond more loosely to the network of social relationships, as they now exist'.

But, just like the high rises, isolated sculptures strewn across large green spaces, the lifting up of streets into the air did not really work out. Why? Were the prominent failures of Berlin's Sonnenallee estate, Manchester's Hulme Crescents, and the Smithsons' own Robin Hood Gardens in East London – the latter two were eventually demolished – due to some structural flaw in the ideas of streets-in-the-sky and deck access? Or did the actual cause, as with other supposed social-housing disasters in the twentieth century, simply come down to systematic under-financing?

The partial success of similar contemporary endeavours, such as Park Hill in Sheffield, would suggest the latter, as would the arguably complete success of earlier projects like the Justus van Effen complex in Rotterdam (which, however,

Barbican: Even with generous spaces – as in London's Barbican – dreams for streets-in-the-sky remained unfulfilled.

did not feature high-rises). Even there, though, the spaces created in the sky were obviously much more confined than any actual street; every street-in-the-sky, unlike city streets on the ground, necessarily has to stop somewhere. As Kenneth Frampton pointed out, it always proved difficult to establish any continuity between decks in the air and streets on the ground.[19] Most obviously, and tragically: one cannot fall from a street, but one can fall from a street-in-the-sky: in 1974 a four-year-old boy died after losing his balance on the top floor of Hulme Crescents.

Some of Jacobs' insights about how streets become safe further illuminate why streets-in-the-sky failed to live up to their promise: there was generally no reason to keep an eye on them; in fact, there was generally no reason to be on them other than to get from A to B (a different situation than the *Gang*, a kind of balcony-corridor running around a courtyard in nineteenth-century Hungarian houses, where you could see what was going on in the courtyard – and, basically, spy on your neighbours across the way); they were obviously not bordered by shops, bars, and restaurants (they were usually just wide enough for a milk cart, though the Smithsons had promised that two mothers with strollers could chat to each other and there'd still be space to walk past them);[20] they were too close to apartments to feel public, yet they were often too poorly lit and too windswept to feel like attractive public space. Their fate confirmed Jacobs' argument about the drawbacks of public and private spaces 'oozing into each other' – and ending up as neither.[21]

Other examples of 'street-making' away from traditional streets can be found at the opposite end of the class spectrum: a Silicon Valley Company once tried to capture, or rather engineer, positive street effects when it built an 'internal street' in its company headquarters. It wasn't accessible to just anyone; plus, it remained subject to constant official surveillance. In the end, the experiment was declared a failure; it did not lead to anything like spontaneous sharing of ideas or community-building among employees (never mind that too much community-building by employees or workers is not always exactly seen as positive by employers to begin with).[22]

The benefits of street life were apparently also intended to materialize on the 'campus' of the pharmaceutical company Novartis in Basel; the vast, privately owned area right next to the river Rhine – dotted with edifices by starchitects like Frank Gehry and Herzog & de Meuron – features privately owned streets, cafés, and plenty of moveable chairs on open squares; that space is partially and at certain hours open to the public. Whether the design had the intended effects of sparking ideas through unplanned encounters or even more ambitious ones of corporate community-building is anyone's guess; what does seem visible, though, is a clear difference between tourists and workers, and the relative absence of regular city inhabitants as such.[23]

The Uses of Mutual Indifference

There's an important feature of city life – villages are a different matter – that is very much in tension with the arguments explored so far. That matters because the feature in question has its own moral and political weight; it is not merely some unfortunate obstacle that we should all work to remove. It's this: a major promise of city life is that presence in the same place does *not* have to mean that encounter in turn should compel anything like meaningful engagement. City streets are ones where presence is barely acknowledged (we lower our head by about ten degrees as we walk on streets);[24] the art of street walking is precisely composed of a skill set that allows us *not* to bump into other people (as confirmed by New Yorkers snapping 'you don't know how to walk' at tourists or suburbanites) and consciously to *avoid* anything that could count as meaningful contact. The German social theorist Georg Simmel, writing at the beginning of the twentieth century, captured the mentality of the city street user with the term *blasé*; he also highlighted that people do relate to each other on the street – indifference is not ignorance or, for that matter, total separation – but with a particular quick glance that is based on a distinct norm: to look for too long is to violate the norm. An invisible 'veil of silence' separates street users.[25]

Being *blasé*, according to Simmel, was partly a matter of self-protection: the sheer number of stimuli in the enormous city could otherwise overwhelm individuals, an element of nineteenth-century speculative psychology one might want to discard.[26] But, in a more plausible vein, Simmel also argued that indifference would create increased space for individuality: precisely because others are not supposed to engage one, self-expression that might give rise to animosity in smaller places can be afforded without fear; and a carefully curated self-presentation tends to draw attention without too much risk. Given the short attention spans of street encounters, there is an incentive to make self-presentation ever more extravagant.

The norm of the quick glance – and moving along fast, what Lorca called the 'furious rhythm' of the big city – are not just matters of psychological self-shielding; they are also grounded in a modern imperative to keep busy, and to get somewhere.[27] At least in the United States, the quintessential question about someone's identity remains 'what do you do?'; it's certainly not 'who are you?' Getting and spending in a world through which we're rushing, the often enough brutal indifference to the fate of others, what a nineteenth-century liberal like Mill described as 'the trampling, crushing, elbowing, and treading on each other's heels' – that all happens primarily in the city.

And it might be happening now more so than ever. A study by scholars at the Massachusetts Institute of Technology compared the films of city sidewalks that Holly Whyte and collaborators had taken with Super-8 cameras in 1980 with recordings of the same places today. The result: 'lingering' decreased by 14 per cent; meanwhile walking speeds increased by 15 per cent. The researchers also found 'a substantial decrease in the amount of group formation'. In short: increasingly, streets are just walkways; they function less and less as social spaces.[28]

But, for some, that had never been the point; rather the promise of the city had been anonymity, or something like *privacy in public*. Virginia Woolf, in her essay on 'Street Haunting', captured the exhilaration of leaving a known self behind as one joins what she called 'that vast republican army of anonymous trampers'; she also observed the liberating effect of indifference, or even superficiality: 'The eye is not a miner, not a diver, not a seeker after buried treasure. It floats us smoothly down a stream; resting, pausing, the brain sleeps perhaps as it looks.' Here is Benjamin's state of distraction turned into a pleasure of sorts.

Of course, street norms have never applied universally. Whoever is somehow vulnerable, or not considered a full citizen, is even more vulnerable, and taken less seriously, on the streets. Up until the twentieth century, women walking the streets alone were assumed to be servants or prostitutes; today, catcalling and the casual brush against female bodies (if not worse) remain a widespread reality, even if condoning them explicitly is becoming taboo.[29] That is not even to mention the blatant inequality of attention exhibited by authorities: stop-question-and-frisk is experienced as a major form of harassment that reinforces existing hierarchies and racism; less obviously, it also goes against norms of privacy in public: just who are the police to question someone in Woolf's republican army of anonymous trampers as to who they are?[30]

The norms associated with the city as a place for being

busy (and being instrumental in one's thinking and conduct), a place where what John Ruskin called 'the Goddess of Getting-on' is being served, have long provoked counter-norms. But these are in no way norms inspired by nostalgia for the village community: the nineteenth-century *flâneur* – according to Baudelaire a 'passionate spectator' setting up house in the heart of the multitude – removed himself from the imperative of getting and spending; the twentieth-century Situationists, artists intent on subverting modern consumer societies, followed the example of the *flâneur* by letting themselves 'drift' aimlessly through the city.

Theirs was a specific resistance to the rationally planned city focused on getting from A to B most efficiently. Le Corbusier hated the sidewalk/pavement, and sidewalk cafés in particular ('a fungus that eats the pavements of Paris'); he also loathed winding streets that, as he put it, merely reflected the old, blind paths that donkeys had once trodden.[31] Modern cities built from scratch – most infamously Brasília, in the eyes of that capital's critics – did not feature winding streets at all; brutal 'systematization' projects as in Communist-ruled Bucharest also ended up creating cities for cars, not for ambling pedestrians. It was, among other things, this 'anti-street'-attitude of modernists that provoked the counter-argument for streets-in-the-sky by the Smithsons and others.

The street becoming more and more like the road meant a systematic shrinking of spaces in which one might encounter others, if one wanted to transcend the norms of acting blasé. Above all, it meant fewer of the surprises that the city might hold – be it just the argument between husband and wife on the street, or actors in street theatre seeking a public; or just getting a glimpse of strangers being exceedingly strange in dress or manners; or just experiencing the street, at a most basic level, as a site of resistance – not in the sense of open rebellion against the powers-that-be, but as a space that is unpredictable, that actually demands alertness, and that might, in a good way, end up foiling our (rational and efficient) plans for the day.

Now, the subversive drifting of the *flâneur* and the Situationists does not make good on the idea that the street is a site for democracy because that's where we experience the demos in its diversity, nor that it can serve as a starting point for democratic community-building. *Flâneurs* do not spontaneously encounter others on the streets, let alone fall into conversation with them; without any focal point – be it observing children (one's own, not those of others) in the playground, or lining up in a queue at the bakery – any attempt by *flâneurs* to 'meet' may well be perceived as bizarre, if not an outright threat.

Jacobs extolled 'eyes on the street' as one of the major advantages of organically grown city life. Neighbours and shopkeepers who knew each other, and each other's kids, would keep streets safe through informal surveillance; what Jacobs called 'the sidewalk and street peace' would be kept primarily not by police, but by 'an intricate, almost unconscious, network of voluntary controls and standards among the people themselves, and be enforced by the people themselves'.[32] People would attract people (the point urbanist Holly Whyte made time and time again: people, strange as it might sound, like to engage in what Whyte called 'self-congestion'); the street would only be worth watching, if there was a lot going on: interesting shops, bars, and restaurants could ensure that. The people not only had to enforce their own safety;

they also had to provide their own entertainment – yet again, something's that unlikely to happen in small, necessarily very confined spaces way up in the sky.

But then again: this portrayal of safety in numbers and through surveillance – with people taking some minimal responsibility for each other in public – would appear to be based on something like a projection of the village, or perhaps suburbia, into the city. Some of neighbourly streets' lauded advantages – encounter with all kinds of different peoples – would then appear at least to be in tension with each other, for safety would seem to result precisely from automatic *mistrust* of locals vis-à-vis strangers to the neigh-bourhood. The places where one can easily separate locals and strangers are the village, the small town, suburbia.

Yet Jacobs herself was adamant that cities were not just larger towns, let alone versions of suburbia; in fact, she insisted, the mistake of modernist city planners had pre-cisely been to aim for a suburbanization of the city, placing its inhabitants in large, supposedly very legible spaces like parks, instead of enjoying diverse, busy, sometimes hard-to-figure-out streets. She may well have conceded that parts of cities would ideally have village-like characteristics, while holding on to the categorical difference between suburbs and cities. For one of the less-noted features of 'the streets of success-ful city neighbourhoods', according to Jacobs, was a 'clear demarcation between what is public space and what is private space' – as opposed to public and private space 'oozing into each other' (as we saw, another possible flaw with streets-in-the-sky). She also regarded this 'oozing' as typical for 'suburban settings' and, less obviously, the 'projects' – which is to say: social housing.[33]

Anonymity is a major promise of the street; city life, in which we remain strangers to each other, can afford what the political theorist Iris Marion Young called 'difference without exclusion' and 'openness to unassimilated otherness'.[34] Young defined city life as a 'being together of strangers'. Privacy is about being in control when it comes to revealing information about ourselves, and when it comes to the degree to which one wants to remain a stranger – and the street is one site for exercising precisely that sort of control.[35] *Not being known* can be an important precondition for self-invention or re-invention; again, one of the major promises of the city: become something new.[36] Anonymity co-exists with the diversity of lifestyles and offerings of what one potentially might want to become – a distinctive feature of city life: as Kahn put it, a city is a place where a child discovers what they want to be. For that promise of self-development to become real, lifestyles just have to be visible and comprehensible enough; to look at someone's self-fashioning and become inspired by it, I do not necessarily have to have exact, let alone extract, data about them; and of course they do not owe me an account of who they are, let alone how and why they became the particular people they are. One might be intimately inspired by total strangers; this is not a contradiction.

In the same way, the tension between what Erving Goffmann called civil inattention and studied indifference on the one hand and, on the other, democratic community-building is relative.[37] The advantage of city life is that those with identities unpopular in smaller, less tolerant places can find each other and engage in forms of solidarity, and, indeed, community-building – which is not to say that they must always cease being strangers, let alone live up to Rousseauean ideals of people being fully transparent to each other.[38] Particular streets might eventually become associated with particular minorities, and some of Dewey's vision may well be vindicated in neighbourhoods where it is known that streets are safe for unpopular minorities.

This sense of 'unassimilated otherness' – to invoke Young again – is just about compatible with a weak version of Jacob's idea of surveillance: people watching over busy streets, but only to make sure nothing obviously dangerous is happening. It's not compatible, however, with the stronger version of the role occupied by local shopkeepers or other members of the 'voluntary network' Jacobs celebrated: they really know people; they have very specific standards as to what kind of people either belong in the neighbourhood or else become automatically suspicious – and, in the eyes of the 'volunteers', make themselves liable for harassment or outright hostility by locals.

I've sought to relativize some conventional claims about street life for democracy in light of a contending moral argument for a particular form of privacy in public. That does not mean all claims for streets as sites of community-building are wrong. But these arguments are strongest when linked to another function of streets beyond the ones concerning encountering diversity: the street as a privileged site for protest. Protests are of course not just about strengthening solidarity and crafting political communities, but they can have these as side-products. Protests, especially acts of civil disobedience, consciously break with the contract of mutual indifference; as we already saw in the discussion of squares, they are about wanting to be in the faces of others, bothering them, disrupting their blasé city routines – not least by taking advantage of the fact that the 'vital organs of the city' – recall Jacobs's designation of the streets – cannot be avoided.

Streaming and Blocking

An image of the street at least as powerful as that of a space of encountering a diverse citizenry – and one with a much longer history – is that of the street as effectively unpredictable and, ultimately, uncontrollable for the powers-that-be. As Jacobs observed, 'if density and diversity give life, the life they breed is disorderly'. Leonard Cohen, in the line preceding his take on the races meeting, had sung that democracy, if at all, was 'coming from the sorrow in the street'.

The anxiety about the street as a source of political sorrow and trouble is an ancient one: Plato compared the masses to a beast and to spoiled children; he also had a sense – wide-spread among critics of Athenian democracy – of assemblies becoming like a kind of uncontrollable flood through the streets.[39] L'Enfant, when planning Washington, DC as a Versailles for a republic, was anxious about 'clotting of the streets'; he wanted to preserve 'spatial dignity' for ceremonial parades on Pennsylvania Avenue (while the Mall was intended for military drills).[40] But streets tend to end up as a dynamic space; the people – and the opinions that dynamic space produced – might unpredictably flow this way or that way; recall Woolf's eye floating 'us smoothly down a stream'. She also noted that the republican army 'of human beings may rouse itself and assert all its oddities and sufferings and sordidities'.

In ancient Athens, access to the street could not be

controlled in the way access to the theatre, the assembly, and the agora could be regulated. Masses on an easily accessible square who have already assembled might be easier to reckon with; often enough, one knows why they are there, who might be responsible for their being there – and that getting them out of the square might be enough to tame a situation politically. After the passing of the 1714 Riot Act in the British Parliament, 'reading the Riot Act' literally meant reading an assembly into illegality, as a group of people was addressed by an official who declared the assembly to be an (illegal) riot; if they failed to disperse, they could then be arrested. It's much harder to read anything to moving people in streets, swarming and streaming along as the authorities try to get in a word.[41] The racist cliché of the 'Arab Street' still contains this sense that opinion-formation is unruly and overly emotional; the notion of an 'Arab Square' would already imply some more control and predictability.

Whether the street is more of an 'echo chamber' than the square is a contingent matter; what's certain is that streets are usually clearly bounded in ways that can be turned into an advantage by those seeking to engage in protest or even political resistance to authorities. The dense university district in northeastern Beijing allowed those bent on organizing a pro-democracy movement in 1989 to use the relatively protected streets to appeal to potential allies in the dorms, agitating in and between the various university complexes without becoming immediately noticeable for the authorities; the appeals put pressure on students to join, and as everyone could see more and more people coming out to take part in the protests, pressure increased further.[42] In other words, the street, rather than automatically being a space for openness and diversity, can also be a site for conspiracy. Or, to use a less loaded term, forming a closely coordinated, and in a sense precisely not very diverse, political will; it can provide shelter and protection from authorities, much more so than the square, be it open or closed.

The most obvious instance of this logic is the erection of barricades to block streets. Barricades date back to the Wars of Religion; in 1588, Parisians tried to block the entry of Henri III's troops, with barrels. The very word barricade derives from the French *barrique*, or barrel.[43] Barricades have been put together spontaneously from the most variegated materials, including cobblestones, newspapers, tyres, dead horses, and bags of ice (during the EuroMaidan in 2014), as well as omnibuses and e-scooters. Some of the materials added symbolic meaning to acts of political defiance: cobblestones were closely associated with the French monarchy; ripping out the *pavé du roi* added insult to injury of royalist troops.

Barricades hardly ever had a decisive practical effect in confronting authorities; they were associated with mass insurrections and resistance movements much more than with successful revolutions. Even though they constituted an exclusively French phenomenon for two hundred years, they hardly appeared in the French Revolution. Belgians, at the end of the 1780s, were the first to use them outside the Hexagon.[44] Their tactical logic is close to that of guerilla warfare: the authorities have to take the barricades in order to win; all that those manning them, in order to prevail, have to do is hold them.

Their defensive nature made them no less feared by state forces, however: military barracks were put in the middle of cities like Vienna and Budapest in the nineteenth century to have soldiers ready to confront the unruly. Paris had seen barricades go up nine times in the period before the Second Empire; during the July Revolution in 1830 alone, 4,000 barricades had been erected (roughly one for every 200 Parisians).[45] These barricades would not only stop, but also trap troops and police; people then threw stones from windows or poured boiling water onto the streets.

Eugène Haussmann, Napoleon's III's prefect of Paris, famously created boulevards – that is to say, massively widened roads – to make blocking by barricade more difficult; macadam replaced cobblestones; and enlargement made it easier to move the military around. Contemporaries took note of the logic behind the *embellissement stratégique*: Flaubert observed in his *Dictionary of Accepted Ideas*, 'Macadam: has cancelled revolutions. No more means to make barricades. Nevertheless rather inconvenient'.[46] And arch-reactionary Louis Veuillot observed apropos the ambiguous liberalism of the latter period of Napoleon III's Second Empire: 'On one hand, they wanted to favor the circulation of ideas, on the other to ensure the circulation of regiments'.[47]

Other than 'installing anti-insurgency hardware into the city',[48] they also wanted to chase the working class out of the city's centre; Haussmann's projects amounted to a gigantic form of real estate speculation, and the 1871 Paris Commune constituted not just a short-lived anarchist experiment featuring around 900 barricades; it also signalled the return of the workers to the centre and, arguably, revenge for their dispossession.

Already by the mid-nineteenth century, observers

questioned whether the barricade still held any practical meaning at all – despite increasingly sophisticated constructions. Gottfried Semper, professor and court architect in Dresden, designed a barricade during the 1849 uprising; it proved difficult to conquer, but was eventually destroyed – as a result, Semper had to go into exile, together with his friend and fellow rebel Richard Wagner (the construction of his famous opera house in Dresden had to be supervised by his son Manfred).[49] Friedrich Engels, one-time 'inspector of barricades' in the Elbersfeld insurrection of the same year, argued that, in the face of reactionary innovations, the barricade's primary meaning was now *moral* rather than military – a point to be echoed by Leon Trotsky. Barricades symbolized bravery and the will to hold out among insurrectionists, and, not least, a will rather to destroy one's possessions – and one's neighbourhood – than put up with further oppression.[50]

Not only revolutionaries saw diminishing practical value in the barricade: the reformist German Social Democratic leader Eduard Bernstein observed early in the twentieth century that 'the barricade fight as a political weapon of the people has been completely eliminated due to changes in weapon technology and cities' structures'; yet, he insisted, some of the ideals behind barricade combat might still inform the workers' movement.[51] Bernstein was also picking up on the fact that, in the era of industrialization, contention unfolded at least as much on the factory floor as on the streets; the strike, not the food riot, became the paradigmatic form of conflict, as the price of labour, rather than the price of goods, caused people to confront the powerful.[52] Blocking production itself grew more important than blocking the street.

However, class conflict was never reducible to demands for better wages and improved working conditions. Alongside – sometimes instead of – a politics of petition there always existed a politics of prefiguration. Squares, one would think, are far more suitable for prefigurative politics: as we saw in the first chapter, they allow for the creation of cities within cities, camps, sometimes even fortresses, that seek to showcase different ways for human beings to relate to each other. Yet theorists of the barricade have tried to argue that barricades can sometimes accomplish the same: they are encampments of sorts or stages.

Stages for what? In the nineteenth century they allowed women to play a particularly important role, very visibly disrupting gender conventions: during the Paris Commune, women built barricades and fired from them, rather than just taking care of the wounded. Barricades can be spectacular; they showcase spontaneous cooperation (some could be put together in only about fifteen minutes). Tocqueville observed in streets close to the Hôtel de Ville in June 1848: 'I found the people engaged in making barricades; they proceeded in their work with the competence and regularity of an engineer, not unpaving more stones than were necessary to lay the foundations of a very thick, solid and even neatly built wall.'[53] During the Gezi Park protests in Istanbul in 2013, one barricade featured a team of drummers.

Barricades are an anonymous creation demonstrating solidarity among strangers: after all, who knows the architect of a barricade? Well, in one famous instance, we do: the largest barricade of the Paris Commune was named after its creator Napoléon (sic!) Gaillard: the 'Château-Gaillard'. There's a photograph of Gaillard proudly standing in front of the massive structure, which blocked the way between the Place de la Concorde and Rue de Rivoli, the street created under the more famous Napoleon. Little did Gaillard know: the French army was able simply to march around the Château.[54]

For enthusiasts of the barricade today, the blocking structures are said to provide spaces where protestors and police might possibly get talking; they create a stage that can also work like a social condenser, even 'a machine to produce the people' (Trotsky also thought soldiers and revolutionaries would end up fraternizing).[55] That might be one reason why military technology has evolved such that the authorities do not even have to get close to the barricade: tear gas was first deployed against those on barricades (before it was used in the First World War); so-called riot-control vehicles can ever more easily crush barricades.[56]

The conclusion appears to be: streets – even if transformed into theatres of sorts through barricading – are hardly the most plausible spaces for prefigurative politics. A demonstration going through streets *streams* from point A to point B, communicating a particular message to a larger, more or less contingent audience of bystanders: the German writer Peter Weiss remarked apropos the student protests of the 1960s: 'The street is our mass medium.' It trades off attention in more places against the permanence of a fixed locale that allows for the continuous showcasing of, let's say, mutual aid, free libraries, diverse deliberative assemblies, or whatever is being created to prefigure an alternative to contemporary society. Continuous community-building is just better accomplished on the square – but something like solidarity generated by continuous joint action is also plausibly realized with people streaming through streets. By streaming – but also blocking! – one also encounters citizens who could easily avoid an encampment on a square; instead, protestors can confront them, engage with them, try to win them over to a cause.[57] Both streaming and blocking can make good on some of the advantages of the street identified by theorists of democracy – but much, much more so in moments of intense protest.

Today, blocking is again prominently associated with street protests. Members of Insulate Britain and Germany's Last Generation super-glue themselves to street surfaces in order to stop car traffic and draw attention to the climate emergency; they have also attached themselves to airport runways and engaged in other spectacular actions, such as sawing off the tip of Berlin's official Christmas Tree.[58] In one sense the *Klima-Kleber* form a human barricade; they immobilize traffic by making themselves immovable. As in the nineteenth century, the meaning of that kind of barricade is moral, not military.

In line with classic accounts of civil disobedience, the willingness to be arrested (by definition, those glued to the pavement cannot escape) and serve prison time – and the willingness to be exposed to the brutality of car drivers who have sometimes tried forcibly to remove those glued to the streets – demonstrates one's moral seriousness. Today's protestors have made themselves consciously vulnerable – unlike the nineteenth-century insurrectionists using barricades for protection; they de facto heed the advice of the American civil-rights leader Bayard Rustin who held that 'the only weapons we have are our bodies, and we need to tuck them in places so wheels don't turn'.

This fearlessness in voluntarily making oneself vulnerable might increase the likelihood of a majority of citizens coming to appreciate the cause that practitioners of civil disobedience are pursuing. For those willing to take the risk of attaching themselves to the street, streaming – in the sense of demonstrations, even very unpredictable ones – is no longer politically sufficient. It draws too little attention and does not compel a reaction; only blocking will do. Blocking also makes for direct confrontations, often angry ones. Obviously, there is no guarantee that an angry citizen will join a cause, but being in the face of others gives protestors at least a fighting chance to persuade them. The same holds for scenarios of demonstrations versus counter-demonstrations; as Jane Jacobs and Holly Whyte had known all along, more people will attract more people, and that makes for at least some increase in potentially receptive audiences.

Today, blocking can be accomplished with highly mobile structures; like the barricade of the nineteenth century, they can be quickly assembled and yet are difficult to move; unlike old-style barricades, however, they can also be swiftly disassembled and be removed and possibly hidden by those who have the engineering and architectural know-how. Think of super tripods and intricate 'protest beacons' based on tensegrity principles; they allow protestors to suspend themselves high above the ground such that special police units have to be brought in to get them down – that lengthens the period of a blockade. In theory, someone could also give a speech from such a position – perhaps reminiscent of the 'Lenin Tribune' that El Lissitzky and Ilya Chashnik designed after the Russian Revolution: mobile, tilted staircases from which the revolutionary masses might be addressed. (Lissitzky and Chashnik also envisaged a screen behind the revolutionary rhetor to display words and images.)[59]

Tripods and beacons are intricate structures; but much

simpler ones can also be highly effective: in 2019 protestors in Hong Kong filled streets with little archways made from just three ordinary bricks: two standing upright, one resting on top. When touched, the falling top one would buttress the other two, and effectively block traffic.[60] In line with their imperative of 'Be Water', protestors would retreat when the police appeared; but the 'mini-Stonehenges' would remain and slow down the authorities.[61]

The past decade also saw the appearance of strange shiny objects on streets filled with protestors: large inflatable cobblestones made of reflective silver-foil, pioneered by the artists-cum-activists of 'Tools for Action'.[62] These objects are highly flexible; they protect against police batons; they pose an awkward challenge to the authorities who often end up looking ridiculous when dealing with them. In addition, as one of its inventors pointed out, they are guaranteed to create a media spectacle. Something also true of the nineteenth-century barricade: people posed for pictures in front of them; these images then helped the police to find Communards and mete out punishments after the brutal end to the short-lived anarchist experiment.[63]

Roads that radicals might want to target are not just ones in fancy post-industrial downtowns; rather, they might block the arteries leading to 'fulfilment centres' and harbours with container shipping. The model would not be so much Occupy Wall Street, which had initially called for the erection of 'peaceful barricades', but the Occupy movement that led to the Port of Oakland shutdown in Northern California in 2011: in short, the roads that cross what geographer Phil Neel has called a 'hinterland' which is barely visible, yet crucial for contemporary capitalism.[64]

Note how a practice sometimes seen as a contemporary version of the barricade – burning cars – has a very different logic.[65] This would virtually never appear to have the moral effects associated with the barricade, or the blocking of the streets undertaken by today's *Klima-Kleber*; after all, the latter can be engaged, and remain answerable, as they have to stay in place. Unlike with those volunteering their own posses-sions to contribute to building a barricade, nobody sets fire to their own car; in fact, it is more likely that people would set fire to their own body – acts of self-immolation have long been part of a repertoire of protest relying on the moral effects of the ultimate self-sacrifice (one need only think of Jan Palach and Alice Herz). The burning car says something, to be sure. But, unlike streaming and blocking, it does not make good on any democratic promises of the street.

The Other Eyes on the Street

Authoritarians distrust streets, or at least small streets, in which people act unobserved and might become harder to find: King Ferdinand declared the narrow streets of Naples a danger to the state as such;[66] Mao's China prevented the pub-lication of detailed street maps.[67] Wherever possible, states have sought to replace irregular streets with grids and large straight streets – in the process offering more or less plaus-ible justifications: Fascists lauded *la linea diretta* as a symbol of decisiveness, and as 'the straight line that does not lose itself in the meanders of Hamlet-like thought'.[68] Above all, they tried to make cities legible from a bird's-eye view (which, sometimes, was effectively the view of an absolute ruler);

that ambition is obviously fulfilled in our day through police helicopters and, increasingly, drones.[69] Haussmann disliked arcades not only because they were growing in unplanned ways, but also because they made for semi-private spaces well-suited to engaging in political conspiracy. Protest movements need safe spaces to meet away from the eyes of the authorities, to plan, and to regroup. These could be private homes, but many homes will not necessarily be, or at least feel, safe.

Then again: if one is planning nothing illegal, and has nothing to hide anyway, why safe spaces, why that incessant clamouring for anonymity? In fact, is the latter not fundamentally opposed to democratic intuitions about visibility and, ultimately, accountability, for which, as we saw earlier, visibility is a precondition, though not a guarantee? People seeing each other clearly mattered a great deal for the ancient Athenians, as we also noted; the sun was supposed to shine onto and entirely illuminate the face of speakers in a democracy. But could *hiding* also be an important affordance of the built environment, and streets in particular?

To be sure, democracy as understood today officially provides spaces for secrecy. The voting booth is the most obvious one; Hannah Arendt found it problematic precisely because it allowed citizens to evade the glaring light of publicity. In what the French call *isoloir*, one has a democratic dialogue at most with oneself, and, above all, one's political decision does not become visible other than through forming part of an aggregate; one certainly is not accountable for it (unlike the politicians sitting quietly in the 'contemplation spaces' of the Scottish Parliament designed by Enric Miralles).

Even philosophers not hankering after the glories of ancient democracy and the glaring light of the *Pnyx* have found this arrangement – secrecy without accountability – problematic. Open voting, John Stuart Mill argued, would improve democratic decision-making; he declared that 'when the voter's own preferences are apt to lead him wrong, but the feeling of responsibility to others may keep him right, not secrecy, but publicity, should be the rule'.[70]

But who are the others to whom one would be 'responsible'? For one thing, they could be those in a position to penalize us for what they consider our wrong decisions: bosses, or the patriarch of the family. Whether they would really do so is beside the point; the very sense of the possibility might alter our decision.[71]

There's a good reason why the US Supreme Court has affirmed a right to anonymity for those engaged in political activity also outside the *isoloir*, in plain public sight. An elderly lady handing out leaflets about a proposed school tax in Ohio in 1988 had insisted on her right not to reveal her identity. The Ohio Supreme Court initially ruled against her, but, as briefly mentioned in the first chapter, the US Supreme Court, pointing out that the *Federalist Papers* had appeared under fictitious names, ruled in her favour. The judges argued that 'anonymous pamphleteering . . . [has] an honorable tradition of advocacy and of dissent. Anonymity is a shield from the tyranny of the majority.' They went on to explain that 'it . . . exemplifies the purpose behind the Bill of Rights, and of the First Amendment in particular: to protect unpopular individuals from retaliation and their ideas from suppression at the hand of an intolerant society'.

In a well-functioning democracy one should not have to

worry about holding unpopular opinions, and one should have no reason to fear sanctions for planning protests. But, of course, many democracies do not function that well. And even in relatively decent ones, it is forgivable to have worries about being penalized for a political stance, be it by public or by private entities.

Even where threats really are very unlikely to materialize, protected spaces are nevertheless important because they allow for reflection and for experimentation with ideas. A space to retreat, the shadows of arcades and the stoa in ancient Athens, for instance (not to speak of the room of one's own in a home), are a physical precondition for eventually asserting a public role in the glaring light of democratic assemblies. Even Hannah Arendt, fierce critic of bourgeois notions of privacy and greatly concerned about the modern retreat from political engagement, conceded that 'a life spent entirely in public, in the presence of others, becomes, as we would say, shallow. While it retains its visibility, it loses the quality of rising into sight from some darker ground which must remain hidden if it is not to lose its depth in a very real, non-subjective sense.'[72] That 'darker ground' might be the room one commands in one's own home. But it could actually also be the streets.

Obviously, streets are not the prime site for ensuring privacy. But streets have become spaces for invasions of privacy that we do not so easily suspect. Seemingly innocuous forms of infrastructure such as LinkNYC – the kiosks that allow people to charge their phones and obtain all kinds of information – constitute integral parts of surveillance capitalism.[73] The supposedly free service exists to monetize the information provided by the person on the street: we think we are getting information; in fact, we are gifting it. Not only that; the increasingly transparent citizen on the street is likely to be steered by search engines as well as maps and other applications in particular ways.[74] The project by Sidewalk Labs (part of Google) to create its own city on the Toronto waterfront – advertised as an 'inclusive urban development' – intended to take this logic to an extreme: it would have required users to use Google apps, in particular its mobile payment system; and it would have provided the company with a 'lab' constantly to observe – and, eventually, to predict – human behaviour.

CCTV cameras, whose effects on street safety are not nearly as evident as their advocates make them out to be, add yet another form of surveillance, not to speak of IMSI-catchers and other technologies of which most citizens are completely unaware.[75] We have our eyes less and less on the streets (and instead on our screens). But the street constantly has its eyes on us. And that is the case even before AI glasses with facial recognition are introduced (and facial recognition is combined with instant information about a person we are looking at); then any expectation of anonymity in public would seem to be finished.[76]

The seeing street creates novel dilemmas for protestors. They have every reason to leave their smartphones at home; but not having a phone also means that they cannot easily coordinate actions on the streets, or, for that matter, film police violence.[77] As briefly discussed in the first chapter, the technology changes the moral calculus: putting one's body at risk at a protest used to be valued as a sign of serious commitment; today, one might not risk life and limb while sitting at home at a computer, but nevertheless endure levels of exposure, as one is being tracked invisibly, that also demonstrate moral seriousness; the problem is that such demonstrations might not be legible as such for other citizens willing to engage in protest (nor, for that matter, impress the authorities very much). Protestors in the American civil-rights movement willing to have the dogs of Southern police forces unleashed on them; me being willing to be tracked online – the very idea of a comparison seems frivolous.

We have seen that the notion of the street as a site of surprise and spontaneous encounters has always been somewhat oversold; undersold, by contrast, is the story of the street as a space for solitude in public and, possibly, the creation of political possibilities in the shelter of relative anonymity: Hannah Arendt's dark ground. Trading these features away for small conveniences is a bad decision in and for a democracy.

The Disappearing Right to Assemble

Reflections on the street reinforce points we already touched on when discussing the sheer importance of citizens having physical space available for self-expression, protest, and prefigurative politics. Yet assembly has not always been recognized as a fundamental communicative right in democracies. True, it was explicitly acknowledged in the First Amendment of the US Constitution, but it did not feature in the French Revolutionaries' Universal Declaration of Human Rights (Rousseauean suspicions of different people demonstrating for different things undermining civic unity probably played a role); even today, there is no explicit acknowledgement in the

French Fifth Republic's constitution. In the United Kingdom
the enormously influential jurist and constitutional theorist
A.V. Dicey held that 'it can hardly be said that our constitution knows of such a thing as any specific right of public
meetings'; tellingly, the Tumultuous Petitioning Act, dating
to 1661, was repealed only in 1986, under the Conservative
government of Margaret Thatcher.[78]

In all jurisdictions freedom of assembly has been the
basic political liberty most subject to restrictions, and prior
restraint in particular: states find it easier to control space
than to control speech. In many countries a jurisprudence
of free assembly remains distinctly underdeveloped.[79] In the
United States there has not been an assembly case in front
of the Supreme Court for about four decades;[80] jurists are
right to claim that, in any case, there is no genuine separate
assembly jurisprudence in American law. Instead, there is a
tendency to run assembly and association together,[81] and to
subsume everything under a jurisprudence of 'free expression' centred on speaking as the paradigm case for expression. The result: where there is no speech involved, then, by
definition, there cannot be a problem with restricting activities; hence, forms of political participation or self-expression
that are 'speechless' end up being less protected. Think of the
encampments set up by student protestors against the Gaza
war in spring 2024, and the fact that so many of them were
outright prohibited by university administrators who were
making pious statements about free speech at the same time.
In a 1965 decision the Supreme Court had already asserted
that 'we emphatically reject the notion . . . that the First and
Fourteenth Amendment afford the same kind of freedom
to those who would communicate ideas by conduct such as

patrolling, marching, and picketing on streets and highways, as these amendments afford to those who communicate ideas by pure speech'.[82]

What else can assembly be if not just speech? One answer is that it acquires meaning from taking place in particular spaces, or what the legal scholar Timothy Zick has called an 'expressive topography'.[83] In other words, assembly might require not just unrestricted articulations of political views, but finding, or making, particular space for assembly. Again, jurisprudence in the United States has been characterized, on the whole, by a surprisingly restrictive approach: for decades, judges followed the lead of legendary Supreme Court Justice Oliver Wendell Holmes, who had asserted that 'public places' are owned by the government, and that, as a consequence, the government has the right to bar access to such places, just like any other property owner. It was only in the seminal 1939 decision of *Hague v. CIO* that state officials became reclassified as trustees, rather than simple property owners; there was now a presumption that the government should make available for assembly both parks and streets that had been 'time out of mind, immemorially held in public trust for purposes of assembly, communicating thoughts between citizens, and discussing public questions'. Yet the judges added that 'the privilege of a citizen of the United States to use the streets and parks for communication of views on national questions may be regulated in the interest of all; it is not absolute, but relative, and must be exercised in subordination to the general comfort and convenience, and in consonance with peace and good order; but it must not, in the guise of regulation, be abridged or denied.'[84]

Like other jurisdictions, then, the United States allowed

for restrictions on the right of assembly in the name of public order; unlike other jurisdictions, it developed a very rigid categorization of different spaces: according to the 'public forum doctrine', one could distinguish among traditional or quintessential public forums ('time out of mind, immemorially held in public trust for purposes of assembly'); designated public forums where members of the public are in principle welcome and where at least sometimes assemblies have been held; and, lastly, straightforwardly non-public forums.

Note how this approach relies at least implicitly on what one might call spatial originalism: if a particular kind of space has always been held to be one of assembly, assemblies must generally be permissible now; if it has only occasionally been designated for assembly, the protection of the right to assembly is uncertain, or outright revocable; and if a place has 'traditionally' not been considered one for assembly, it appears impossible to assert a right to gather in it. This spatial originalism might not seem to pose much of a problem for public squares or also greens;[85] except that only some might have an unbroken tradition of spaces where the people come together; some might only occasionally have been designated as sites of assembly; and non-traditional places – such as a plaza inside a commercial mall or an airport – would appear to be categorically ruled out as sites of assembly.

Judges in other democracies have been more willing to open up non-traditional spaces for political protest. The German Constitutional Court ruled that the publicly accessible part of Frankfurt Airport – the areas not restricted to ticketed passengers – was a legitimate site of political activity, even if the area was privately owned property devoted to commercial activity (to be sure, the state owning a large part of the airport played an important role in the decision). The Court held that 'the wish to create a "feel-good atmosphere" in a sphere which is strictly reserved for consumer purposes and which remains free from political discussions and social conflicts cannot be used as the basis for prohibiting the distribution of leaflets'. The judges went on to explain that 'the state may not restrict fundamental rights in order to ensure that the carefree mood of citizens is not disturbed by the misery of the world'.[86]

There are ever more subtle forms of weakening the right to assembly, without ever officially disavowing it: high administrative burdens and fees can effectively amount to a tax on free expression and political participation; the politically active have to pay, everyone else gets to use public space for free. Such de facto taxes go against the spirit of assembly being, in the words of a US Supreme Court decision, 'essential to the poorly financed causes of little people'.[87] Costs increase further if organizers face significant risks of civil liability: after the protests following the murder of George Floyd, an African American, by a white police officer in Minneapolis in 2020, some states in the US introduced new, ill-defined grounds for liability such as 'riotboosting' and 'negligent protest organizing'. The latter – a form of liability essentially made up by one of the most Trumpist courts in the country, officially devoted to sticking to the 'original meaning' of the constitution – would have held any organizer responsible for violence at a protest event, even if the organizer had explicitly discouraged violence. In fact, they might even be held responsible for violence from counter-protestors: a Black Lives Matter organizer could go to prison because someone from the KKK threw a rock at a policeman.[88]

A permit regime can serve to institutionalize or 'bureau-cratize' protest and create what critics rightly see as an increasingly rigid 'public order management system'.[89] Such a system diminishes the capacity of those participating to get in the face of other citizens, as they are safely contained in official 'bubbles' and 'free-speech zones' – the flip side of which are speech-free zones.

Do the differences between squares and streets we dis-cussed earlier matter here? Freedom of assembly, as a basic communicative right essential for a democracy, generally covers both. But one conclusion from our discussion is that different urban forms facilitate different kinds of political conduct. We also saw that different places represent different things. In other words, spaces for politics are not interchange-able. And yet every so often, protestors and those intent on practising prefigurative politics have been told by author-ities that they are free to do what they want to do – just not where they want to do it. Sometimes, political conduct is truly place-dependent. Those who care about free assembly should also care to make sure that people are free to assemble (or march) in the right place.

Making Space Hostile

Assemblies might be diverted to undesirable places; they might be prohibited outright – or they might be rendered extremely difficult by changes in the built environment. Moscow's Manege Square – the site of many demonstrations after 1990 – saw the construction of an underground shopping mall, covered by a glass dome, as well as the creation by the notorious sculptor Zurab Tsereteli of a fountain with Russian fairy-tale characters. Tahrir Square in Cairo was 'beautified' after the 2011 Egyptian Revolution with an enormous number of large concrete planters, atop an underground parking garage; this has made mass rallies more difficult (quite apart from the fact that the highly repressive regime would not tolerate them). A monument devoted to the Revolution was officially supposed to bring people together; an obelisk got chosen to symbolize pride in the past and unity (the revolutionaries themselves had erected a makeshift obelisk engraved with the names of those killed by Mubarak's henchmen in 2011). As I discovered on a visit in summer 2023, anyone approaching the monument will immediately be confronted by numerous security guards.

Not everything that functions as hostile architecture, especially architecture hostile to politics, necessarily looks hostile; it can easily be disguised to make cities look greener and more liveable. Some forms of hostility are barely noticeable: armrests or metal pipes are installed in the middle of many benches to make it virtually impossible comfortably to stretch out on them (so as to keep away the homeless); windowsills are sloped so as to prevent people sitting on them; skatestoppers, also known as 'pig ears', are added to ledges. POPOS – privately owned public open spaces – often feature such hostile elements in order to keep out a public legally entitled to be there.

Designers have responded with innovations hostile to hostile architecture, so to speak: the Chicago artist Sarah Ross modified jogging suits to create 'archisuits' which included padding so as to allow one to sit on uneven surfaces and fill the spaces between armrests on benches; she explained that

'The suits . . . allow a wearer to fit into, or onto, structures designed to deny them . . . Archisuits suggest a wearer might resist by not only being present but being present comfortably, leisurely.'[90] Others have placed mattresses over spikes or designed structures for shelter that fold out from benches.[91]

As I said, governments find it easier to control space than to control speech, and authoritarian regimes control spaces in a particularly tight way. They also bet that people might eventually forget what happened in a particular place such that being there loses political significance. In one of the largely forgotten tragedies of the Arab Spring, the oppositional gatherings at Bahrain's Pearl Roundabout – named after the Pearl Monument in its middle – were brutally crushed, mostly at the hands of military forces led by Saudi Arabia. The monument was destroyed – though spectacular footage of its destruction in turn had to be destroyed because a worker had accidentally been killed on camera. The roundabout area was paved over, a statue of a figure detested by the Shia – the oppressed part of the population mainly behind the 2011 uprising – was erected. And yet: the image of the Pearl Monument persisted in graffiti; in fact, people were even willing to go on record to say that they kept dreaming about it.[92]

And Rabaa? Today it is not legible as a square of any kind – since the massacre it has been a large intersection with a flyover, a structure that could easily be used by army snipers in the future. When I visited, there was no problem photographing the large roads – but pictures of the local mosque, which has been closed ever since 2013, had to be deleted. A plainclothes officer with a large weapon ostentatiously displayed felt the need to take me into the military compound next to the mosque (I duly pretended to have deleted all the

The mosque at Rabaa Square. Closed since 2013.

photographs). The mosque, I figured, was the equivalent of the Pearl.

In a disturbingly similar vein, the large security detail that accompanied me into Kahn's parliament building in Dhaka first insisted that images could only be taken with a mobile phone, not with a professional camera; when I snapped a photo of a graffito in the parliament's beautiful library, an officer insisted that it had to be deleted and that, from now on, all photography would be forbidden. Of course, I had had no idea what the graffito meant; it was eventually explained to me that it said 'August 5th is victory day' – in contrast, I suppose, with 16 December, which was the day of Pakistan's defeat in 1971.

Such experiences are not exceptional, maybe not even worth reporting. Except that they show how much governments care about the messages sent by buildings, or by what's on buildings. Message control can be more or less subtle, though. Which brings us back to The Line.

Back to The Line

At the beginning of this book, I briefly mentioned the project of a linear city in the north-western corner of Saudi Arabia. It is unclear what, if anything really, will ever be built; after grand announcements of the kingdom's commitment to this futuristic endeavour, ambitions were suddenly scaled back in spring 2024: instead of 170 kilometres, only 2.4 kilometres would be created by 2030; instead of nine million inhabitants, a mere 300,000 people would supposedly reside in the megastructure by then. In 2025, work apparently stopped altogether.

The idea of a linear city is not new: the Spanish urban planner Arturo Soria y Mata pioneered it in the 1880s. His *Ciudad Lineal* was said to exemplify 'progressive urbanism'; he assumed that commuting times would be shortened as much as possible, and that a linear city could maximize health and well-being.[93] Early in the twentieth century, the American urban planner Edgar Chambless followed with a linear design that featured a street on the roof as well as a monorail and a bicycle path. His ambition was larger still than the Saudis' today: his line was intended to stretch across nothing less than the entire United States, from coast to coast.[94] Despite support from luminaries like Thomas Edison, the project failed completely, and Chambless ended his life with the help of a gas heater, alone in a furnished room in New York City.[95] Proposals for linear cities were also prominent in the Soviet Union; none ever came to fruition. Not least, come to think of it, Schultes and Frank's Federal Ribbon was meant to be a linear city within the city: chancellery, civic forum, and plenty of government buildings would have fitted between two walls, 22 metres high, extending from Moabit to the Friedrichstrasse railway station.[96]

The Line of the Saudis is not just noticeable for promising the proper realization of a long-standing dream. Most remarkably, it picks up design ideas developed by the highly experimental groups Archigram, Archizoom, and Superstudio in the 1960s. The British Archigram members presented avant-garde projects like 'The Walking City' or 'Pop-City', essentially mobile megastructures (the perfect city for the Athenians, come to think of it); the Italian architects of Archizoom proposed the 'No-Stop City'; Superstudio – also Italian – envisaged a large linear structure running across the desert, as well as many other landscapes, entitled 'Continuous Monument'. They all appear to prefigure The Line.

There's a crucial difference, though: Superstudio and Archigram did not create designs as blueprints to be picked up by investors or autocrats; their intention was decidedly satirical and subversive, and critical of consumer capitalism in particular. As they liked to put it, the challenge was to 'inject noise into the system'.[97] 'Continuous Monument' sought to raise the alarm about a potential total urbanization of the globe, which, after all, was bound completely to destroy nature. Superstudio's co-founder Adolfo Natalini proclaimed in 1971: 'If design is merely an inducement to consume, then we must reject design; if architecture is merely the codifying of bourgeois models of ownership and society, then we must reject architecture; if architecture and town planning is merely the formalization of present unjust social divisions, then we must reject town planning and its cities'. To put a complex story in simple terms: Superstudio positioned itself as anti-design, in the name of anti-consumerism and anti-capitalism.

And yet we find exact continuities between the counter-cultural movements of the 1960s and The Line – in terms of self-presentation, but even when it comes to personnel. One of the architects involved in the region of 'Neom' in Saudi Arabia is Peter Cook, a founder of Archigram. Lavishly produced coffee-table books on The Line available at the 'Zero Gravity Urbanism' exhibition in Venice claimed that The Line's inspiration was in fact nothing else but punk. Why? Punk meant maximum disruption of all musical trad-itions; The Line, getting rid of something as basic – some might say constitutive of cityhood – as the street was supposed to maximally disrupt traditional understandings of the city.

While the lavish designs proposed by starchitects vying for realizing the project all highlight 'ubiquitous public realm', in none of the renderings made available so far does there seem to be anything resembling a large square (how could there be in a relatively narrow corridor?), or anything

The Line: The promise is of 'ubiquitous public realm'. But everyone will have to get in line . . . and stay in line.

like a street for that matter. Had there been a circle instead of a line as the basic template, things would have been different; some might also say that corridors – if one thinks of them as a street – can still be sites of protest, including the erection of barricades. But, in principle, certain functions of assembly would be made impossible by the design of The Line – not to mention surveillance or control by security guards.

Linear cities have always required a great deal of control: after all, one cannot build and get out of line if one is required to respect the initial design. If transportation is controlled centrally – as in The Line's proposed super-fast underground connection – people won't be able to rush to a site of protest.[98] Never mind that the project is located in a country governed by a repressive, absolute monarchy; the very design narrows the space for democracy. People will have to get in line and stay in line.

Coda: Seven Building Blocks for Thinking about Architecture and Democracy

1. Humans make their own history, but not in a built environment of their own choosing.[1] In theory, what we inherit we could remake; yet most of the time we don't think all that much about what is already around us, or even really notice it. That was Walter Benjamin's point about humanity always building, and yet also always experiencing architecture in a state of distraction. We see it, and we don't see it – and we probably see things even less today, as we stare down at screens, instead of looking up at buildings. True, one might say the same about certain kinds of background music. Except there isn't always music playing. But there are almost always built structures around us.

The promise of democracy is to realize freedom and equality; yet we often experience the built environment in a state of unfreedom and inequality: most of us will never have the means to remake it beyond, at best, a single house or apartment: we don't have the resources; we also often don't have the authority. Some do, and, in democracies, they are supposed to operate within the limits of laws animated by a collective purpose (such as affordable housing for all citizens).

The fact is that today, perhaps more than ever before in

the history of modern democracy, the built environment has escaped any aspiration to collective control. (Never mind ancient democracy: there is evidence that the building of the Parthenon and other parts of the Acropolis were continuously debated and made subject to decrees by citizens assembled on the *Pnyx*.) Meanwhile, the spaces to express a desire to take back control are shrinking, as the right to assembly is being hollowed out in obvious and sometimes not so obvious ways.

2. In a democracy, political outcomes are uncertain; there is only certainty about *how* we arrive at authorizing some to make collectively binding decisions for the rest of us. The 'how' includes basic political rights – free speech, free assembly, free association – that enable us to show up, and to speak up.[2] In autocracies, it is the other way around: the outcomes are known in advance: everyone knows which person or party will win. But political procedures can be changed – that is to say, manipulated – at any time; rights can be restricted.[3]

Autocracies seek to make the political order as a whole visible, in spectacles carefully choreographed around leaders, while its procedures remain in the dark. Democracies can never show a definitive whole – no symbol can conclusively capture 'the people' once and for all – but democracies do not seek to hide the messy reality of their procedures and decision-making processes.

Democracy allows us to become politically visible to each other; it does not force us to do so. Autocracies, by contrast, tend to force us; Fascism most certainly does: its spectacle of participation is a scripted performance against a given scenography. The young Hitler, contrary to conventional wisdom, was not so much taken with architecture as with theatre design. How people will look at each other under Fascism is predictable – even if the spectacle takes surprising turns to awe audiences. By contrast, people looking at each other in a democracy can yield unexpected outcomes.

Democracy is not one practice, not one thing, and therefore also does not rely on one space. Or one building, for that matter. Enric Miralles, when designing the Scottish Parliament, made a point of saying that he wanted neither a palace nor a dome. Instead, he wanted a campus, an assemblage of buildings with different functions.[4] In a somewhat similar vein, Louis Kahn's parliament building in Dhaka, on the inside, feels like a vast concrete city – a city with variegated grey skyscrapers and different rooms opening up unexpectedly as one explores Kahn's ambulatory.

3. What happens on streets and squares has no democratic form, but it does have democratic meaning.[5] This point is not a variation of the old demophobic prejudice that the masses on streets and squares are inherently 'formless', shorthand for unpredictable, or, if in doubt, irrational and dangerous. As we saw, Tocqueville was particularly anxious about democracy's formlessness; Elias Canetti, the psychologist of crowds, stressed that the fear of crowds is intimately linked to a basic fear of being touched by strangers.

But that fear can be overcome; and informal politics is not shapeless politics. Different shapes come with advantages and disadvantages. An encampment on a square or a barricade in a street means staying in place; you can be found. A march means you go after people where *they* can be found.

Camps enable prefigurative politics: showcasing a particular future you deem desirable. The term derives from the Latin 'campus': an open field for a military exercise – but also a political exercise.[6]

Unlike marches, in which you still follow the conventional imperative of the street – people must keep circulating – an encampment disobeys the imperative of keeping a square as open and accessible as possible.[7] The French *se camper* means to plant oneself firmly in front of something.[8] Despite this fundamental gesture of defiance, shared with the barricade, an encampment might just be a form of protest: a politics of petitioning the powerful (and thereby affirming existing institutions). Marches, by definition, can *only* really constitute a form of protest, even if they are also meant to convey messages beyond immediate complaints. The most famous march in American history, the 1963 March on Washington, was also intended to demonstrate discipline: only preapproved placards with standardized slogans were allowed; even what could be brought for lunch – peanut butter and jelly sandwiches – was centrally decided by civil-rights leaders.[9]

Encampments enable an ambiguous relationship between those not encamping and those encamping: one can move inside the encampment without revealing whether one is really being supportive or not; for all one knows, people moving inside the encampment could be political tourists. Again, the situation with marches is much more clear-cut: you can be part of an audience on the sidewalk, or you can move with the march and hence unambiguously join. There comes a moment when you'll be counted or not.[10]

The ambiguity of one's relation to an encampment is

itself ambiguous as to its political effects: it can make it easier to get engaged (after all, many potential supporters might initially have reservations); it can also make it harder to understand who has truly committed.

Canetti drew a distinction between open and closed crowds. One does not have to adopt his crowd psychology in order to adapt his thought along the lines that there can be open and closed camps, just as there can be open and closed squares (whereas there cannot really be open or closed marches). The open one invites communication; the closed one primarily aims at strengthening internal cohesion. Both might end up functioning as social condensers.

4. Informal practices need formal laws that guarantee political freedom: access to spaces that mean something to people, and permission to get in each other's faces.[11] They also require streets and squares to be maintained well enough.[12] Rousseau observed that 'houses make the city but Citizens make the City'. Yes, but some houses – and spaces – make it easier for Citizens to make the City. Laws enable this process, as does proper financing, as do design choices signalling that citizens are indeed welcome 'to make the City' – think back to Cedric Price's plans for Parliament Square as a site of protest, and think back to the difference that different designs would have made for Brian Haw. Also recall Frieder Schnock's point about memorials saying 'You are someone'. A political building should say the same.

Freedom in a democracy means the freedom to instigate political conflict. Conflict is not the opposite of cohesion; conflict can in fact create cohesion. The German legal theorist Gustav Radbruch once observed that the people could be thought of as a Gothic dome in which 'the masses' support each other by striving in different directions.[13] Conflict can take place – peacefully – on streets, squares, and, of course, inside formal assemblies. The democratic city is not what the greatest anti-democratic theorist, Plato, described as a 'team of horses'[14] – it doesn't pull in one direction, it does not breathe as one. But his point that a city ultimately needs to be on friendly terms with itself also applies to democracies.

This is a serious challenge for democratic design: how to provide adversarial space, so to speak, without knowing which shape conflicts will take, and how – or even whether – conflict will translate into cohesion. Sometimes citizens themselves will come up with the designs for adversarial space: no one had planned roundabouts in rural France to be sites of protest.

5. The built environment both constrains and enables; it also cues us with a continuous flow of direct and indirect messages, including what Schultes, one of the architects of the Berlin Chancellery, called 'suggestive spatiality'.[15] Since the Renaissance, buildings increasingly come with texts, often misleading ones: 'democracy talk' is excellent raw material for more or less false advertising in architecture. Corbusier wrote as many books as he built buildings; his identity card indicated as profession: *homme de lettres*.[16]

Given that the politically active on streets and squares might have posters, but certainly will have mobile phones, all spaces are today multi-media spaces. We keep imagining the internet in spatial terms ('echo chambers'); we also think of it as somehow separate from the 'real world' (though probably no one is still naive enough to think of it as somehow 'neutral'). The internet is not 'less real', and its architecture can in fact be much more solid, or outright implacable, compared to our experience of physical spaces. From online publics, crowds can emerge to occupy physical space; and people on the ground orient their movements with a view to how they will appear online.

The internet upsets conventional divisions between the public and the private: walking among the crowds without a mobile phone, and hoodie pulled down, or wearing a face mask – where still allowed – to avoid recognition technologies, is evidently more private than being sprawled in one's bed, while being tracked across the internet (and possibly being surveilled by the internet of things). Designs for democracy need to think the physical and the virtual together.

6. What takes place on streets and squares is synchronous, though it can also follow a ritual unfolding over time – think of the French left's traditional march from République to Nation in Paris. What goes on inside designated political buildings follows rigid sequencing; such processes make it likely – no guarantees! – that one arrives at collectively binding, that is to say authoritative, decisions.

A place producing authority must be dignified; it does not have to be glorified. At the very least it ought to be legible as something special (unlike the EU's edifices in Brussels). This can be done in many different ways; one must remember, though, that the overriding purpose is to *serve* democratic functions, not to illustrate them or merely, as Boullée had it, 'excite in us sentiments analogous to the functions to which the buildings are devoted'.[17] This can include helpful reminders that *the people* are out there – and that, of course, they have every right and the right space to complain about how they are being represented.

There is no uniquely correct way of shaping the inside of parliaments; different, perfectly valid considerations stressing different aspects of democracy pull in different directions: a desire to dramatize conflicts – so that citizens clearly understand their choices – will yield different configurations from a demand to negotiate in a safe space, based on a *justifiable* lack of access and transparency; but that, in turn, is in tension with an understanding of democracy as centrally concerned with the fight against corruption (recall the Doge's Palace).

'Transparency' is the most overrated and misunderstood concept when architecture and democracy are considered together. Practically, all attempts to make all spaces fully transparent will only result in politicians finding new locations for secrecy; it is better to find a legitimate space for secrecy, just as the dealings in the ancient stoa were accepted as a complement to what happened in full view on the *Pnyx*.

Never mind practice; at the level of theory, accounts of transparency as conventionally understood promise much more for democracy than they can fulfil. An alternative reading of transparency – interpenetration without destruction – is helpful: citizens cannot see all of politics, let alone all of society, but they might just be able to keep an eye on different, partially overlapping elements at the same time – and understand how things do or do not fit together.

Democracy is open-ended and often besieged; but it would be silly literalism to demand that its buildings must be unfinished, let alone that citizens regularly 'storm' 'their house'. Democratic edifices can suggest the solid and the open, the certainty of procedures, and the always uncertain content of democratic politics unfolding within them. This is what made Kahn's parliament surprisingly coherent: a supremely dignified edifice that allows for the unexpected on the inside and contains what Kahn called a 'society of rooms' in which a pluralist politics potentially finds a foothold. Of course, it does not guarantee such a politics. Under the watch of what locals often simply refer to as the Sansad building, Bangladesh kept losing democracy. It should have been obvious all along, but it's worth stating explicitly: political problems do not have architectural solutions (though architectural problems can have political solutions). Kahn's building could not really 'bring democracy'. But it has retained the capacity to represent and facilitate democracy.

7. Just as democracy is not one thing, or one practice, the meaning of democracy cannot be condensed into one symbol. John Quincy Adams was right that democracy is iconographically challenged, so to speak. But this does not mean that democracy is necessarily bereft of visual strategies. One can evoke past heroic democratic action, for instance, and live up to the idea that democratic citizens think for themselves. There's a reason why all images of Bahrain's Pearl Roundabout were destroyed (and yet people kept dreaming of the Roundabout still being there, and of reuniting inside it).

Democracy – as a politics of second thoughts – is more likely to revisit, revise, and recontextualize its iconographic programme. For that reason, it is likely to favour the counter-monument or even the anti-monumental monument, the one that gestures at the broken, the fragmentary, the open, and the *incomplete*. The French historian Jules Michelet's observation is an extreme version of this insight: 'While the Empire had its columns and Royalty had the Louvre, the Revolution had for its monument . . . only the void.'

Citizens themselves will always fill the void anew, remove what's there, and fill it anew.

Notes

INTRODUCTION: THE BUILDING
THAT BROUGHT DEMOCRACY

1. Wendy Lesser, *You Say to Brick: The Life of Louis Kahn* (New York, NY: Farrar, Straus & Giroux, 2017), 255. A whole book could be written about the Sansad, namely Kahn's parliament, and political ideas. Kahn was inspired by the Baths of Caracalla, by Mughal architecture, by the Indian fort tradition, and by local Bengali conditions (especially the role of water); but, above all, he sought to follow his own theory of how architecture could express a particular institution's essence, in this case, the 'transcendent nature' of assembly (something that, in his view, Western civic buildings no longer managed in the twentieth century). It is easy to criticize some of the high-minded rhetoric about democracy and assembly, be it Kahn's own pronouncements or that of his admirers, as hypocritical: he was commissioned by an authoritarian, Pakistan's ruler Ayub Khan, and incorporated a mosque in a way that, for many, would appear to violate the separation of state and religion – while also getting the orientation of the mosque wrong. (Kahn stated flatly: 'I thought the mosque should be answerable to the assembly and the assembly answerable to the mosque.') The most trenchant critique can be found in Lawrence Vale, *Architecture, Power, and National Identity*, 2nd ed. (New York, NY: Routledge, 2008).

2. Quoted in Carter Wiseman, *Louis Kahn: A Life in Architecture* (Charlottesville, VA: University of Virginia Press, 2020), 103.

3. *The New York Times*, on the other hand, likened the edifice to a beached ocean liner.

4. To be sure, only the very final decision had been made by Kohl, who in fact went out of his way to stress that he did not want to create a monument for himself. The jury, after contentious debates, had awarded two first prizes and thought it best to leave the choice to the Chancellor (in the end aided by many experts and journalists). The full story is told in Heinrich Wefing, *Kulisse der Macht: Das Berliner Kanzleramt* (Stuttgart: Deutsche Verlags-Anstalt, 2001).

5. For the official presentation of the project, see: https://www.neom.com/en-us/regions/theline; for a critical overview, see https://www.dezeen.com/2023/02/14/neom-guide-line-saudi-arabia.

6. Oscar Schneider, *Fundamente: Plädoyer für eine menschenwürdige Architektur und Baupolitik* (Stuttgart: DVA, 1986), 162.

7. Minoru Yamasaki, 'Toward an Architecture of Enjoyment', *Architectural Record*, vol. 118 (1955), 142–9; here 149.

8. Daniel Libeskind, 'Learning from the World Trade Center Wrangles', *Wall Street Journal*, 11 November 2013.

9. Quoted in Andrew Rice, 'Big Deal', at: http://www.wired.com/2015/09/bjarke-ingels-2-world-trade-center-wtc-2.

10. Thanks to Danny Abramson for this point.

11. See also Raymond Guess, 'Politics and Architecture', in *A World without Why* (Princeton, NJ: Princeton University Press, 2014), 144–62.

12. Aristotle, *Politics*, trans. C.D.C. Reeve (Indianapolis, IN: Hacket, 2017), 1267b21–1269b28 (pp. 36–40). Hippodamus lived from 498 to 408 BCE; Aristotle may have thought of him as the first urban planner, but there had been millennia of city planning before him (just think of the Chinese nine-square city plans). See Jonathan F.P. Rose, *The Well-Tempered City* (New York, NY: Harper, 2016).

13. It was not a spontaneous thought; Churchill had formed it decades earlier: in 1924, on the occasion of an awards ceremony of the Architectural Association, he pronounced that there 'is no doubt whatever about the influence of

architecture and structure upon human character and action. We make our buildings and afterwards they make us. They regulate the course of our lives.' Stewart Brand, *How Buildings Learn: What Happens after They're Built* (New York, NY: Penguin, 1995), 3.

14. An understanding of the political as association and dissociation was infamously proposed by the Nazi legal theorist Carl Schmitt – but not every such understanding has to come with an authoritarian Schmittian politics.

15. Sarah Schindler, 'Architectural Exclusion: Discrimination and Segregation through the Built Environment', *Yale Law Journal*, vol. 124 (2014–15), 1,934–2,024.

16. Steen Eiler Rasmussen, *Experiencing Architecture* (Cambridge, MA: MIT Press, 1964), 142.

17. This dynamic is not *inherently* connected to monarchy: Georgian houses had a similar spatial dynamic – they moved visitors from front to back, from reception space to music and retiring rooms. Charles Holland, *How to Enjoy Architecture* (New Haven, CT: Yale University Press, 2024), 63. In Versailles, however, it was occasionally the king himself who would usher people along in a particular way: he thought there was *one* correct way of experiencing the gardens of Versailles; he even codified it in writing. See Louis XIV, *Manière de montrer les jardins de Versailles* (Paris: Éditions de la Réunion des Musées Nationaux, 1992).

18. Hannah Arendt, *The Human Condition* (Chicago, IL: University of Chicago Press, 1989), 194. She was discussing Greek political thought and added that, for them, 'legislator and architect belonged in the same category' (*ibid.*, 195).

19. Friedrich Nietzsche, *Götzendämmerung, Kritische Studienausgabe*, vol. 6 (Stuttgart: DVA, 1999), 118–19.

20. Victor Hugo, *Notre Dame de Paris* (Paris: Gallimard, 2009). In the original, the chapter is entitled *Ceci tuera cela*. The mini-treatise, for which Hugo had consulted architects, was included in the second, 1832 edition; at the time, Hugo hoped for a Gothic

revival. Harry Francis Malgrave, *Modern Architectural Theory: A Historical Survey, 1673–1968* (New York, NY: Cambridge University Press, 2005), 80–2.

21. *Ibid.*, 287. For the Nazi approach, see Kurt Rupli's 1939 propaganda film *Das Wort aus Stein*. See also Sharon Macdonald, 'Words in Stone? Agency and Identity in a Nazi Landscape', *Journal of Material Culture*, vol. 11 (2006), 105–26. For the Hitler quote ('Die Steine reden wirklich, wenn die Menschen schweigen'), see Wolfram Pyta, *Hitler: Der Künstler als Politiker und Feldherr – Eine Herrschaftsanalyse* (Berlin: Siedler, 2015), 90.

22. John Parkinson, *Democracy and Public Space: The Physical Sites of Democratic Performance* (New York, NY: Oxford University Press, 2012).

23. Henri Lefebvre, *The Production of Space*, trans. David Nicholson-Smith (Oxford: Blackwell, 1992).

24. Walter Benjamin, 'Das Kunstwerk im Zeitalter seiner technischen Reproduzierbarkeit (Erste Fassung)', *Abhandlungen* [Gesammelte Schriften, vol. I:2], eds. Rolf Tiedemann and Hermann Schweppenhäuser (Frankfurt: Suhrkamp, 1991), 431–69; here 465–6.

25. Lynn Hunt, 'Hercules and the Radical Image in the French Revolution', *Representations*, vol. 1 (1983), 95–117; here 107.

26. The tallest statue in the Western hemisphere can be found in Puerto Rico; it was created by the notorious Georgian sculptor Zurab Tsereteli. He had offered his *Birth of the New World* – featuring Columbus and 110 metres tall – to numerous cities in the mainland US, including New York City; every single one rejected it. Donald Trump at one point tried to have it installed on one of his real-estate developments on Manhattan's West Side.

27. There has been a long-standing debate – starting in the late nineteenth century – whether architecture should primarily be defined as the creation of spaces. We do not need to settle this debate in order to examine why and how particular practices

in a democracy, from debating to demonstrating, require particular kinds of spaces. See August Schmarsow, *Das Wesen der architektonischen Schöpfung* (Leipzig: Karl W. Hiersemann, 1894); Bruno Zevi, *Saper vedere l'architettura* (Turin: Einaudi, 2009 [1948]). Critics might object that such a concentration just reflects a modernist prejudice; Robert Venturi and Denise Scott-Brown, for instance, charged modernism with worshipping 'sacred' or 'deified' space entirely at the expense of symbolism (or, more concretely, ornamentation). But the point remains that certain functions in a democracy necessarily require spaces; what Venturi and Scott-Brown saw as anti-spatial – style, for instance – might help or hinder fulfilling these functions.

28. Quoted in Thomas A. Markus, *Buildings and Power: Freedom and Control in the Origin of Modern Building Types* (London: Routledge, 1993), 123.

29. Xinghai Square in Dalian (with a diameter of 239.9 metres, an allusion to the city's founding date) features an inscription celebrating the unity of the Chinese people.

30. Joan Ockman, 'What Is Democratic Architecture? The Public Life of Buildings', *Dissent*, vol. 58 (Fall 2011), 65–72.

31. *Ibid.*

32. The place for making collectively binding decisions does not have to be a building: think of the annual Icelandic *althingi*, an open area (Thingvellir) with attendees pitching tents.

I SQUARE: USES OF ASSEMBLY

1. *Agoreúô* meant 'I speak in public'; *agorázô* meant 'I shop.' Meanwhile, stones featured a tell-it-as-it-is inscription: 'I am the boundary stone of the agora.'

2. For the argument that the Greek public had three 'poles', see Tonio Hölscher, *Öffentliche Räume in frühen griechischen Städten* (Heidelberg: Universitätsverlag C. Winter, 1998). 'Public' refers to the notions of *demios* and *koinos* – what belongs to the people as a whole (16).

3. *Federalist*, no. 55, in *The New York Packet* (13 February 1788).

4. James Baldwin, *Collected Essays*, ed. Toni Morrison (New York, NY: Library of America, 1998), 376.

5. To be sure, the world of the Greek polis is not reducible to Athens; the stylized account offered here is meant to tell us something about democracy and the built environment, not paint a comprehensive picture of ancient Greece. For a historical overview of the wider context of different poleis, see John Ma, *A New History of the Ancient Greek City-State from the Early Iron Age to the End of Antiquity* (Princeton, NJ: Princeton University Press, 2024).

6. The recent renovation of the parliament in Vienna included the creation of an 'Agora' aimed at educating citizens about their political system; citizens can click on videos of life-size political leaders explaining their understanding of democracy.

7. To be sure, this point is subject to dispute among historians of the ancient world.

8. Irad Malkin and Josine Blok, *Drawing Lots* (New York, NY: Oxford University Press, 2024), 271.

9. Machiavelli was then to claim that the continuous conflict between *grandi* and *popolari* was in fact a safeguard of republican liberty.

10. Jessica Paga, *Building Democracy in Late Archaic Athens* (New York, NY: Oxford University Press, 2020). The wealthy were supposed to distinguish themselves through the sponsorship of plays and festivals; only in Hellenistic times did houses become more opulent (and the large peristyle courtyard a space where public and private came to blend into each other). See Elena Walter-Karydi, *Die Nobilitierung des Wohnhauses: Lebensform und Architektur im spätklassischen Griechenland* (Konstanz: Universitätsverlag Konstanz, 1994).

11. I am grateful to Effie Rentzou for this point.

12. Tonio Hölscher, *Öffentliche Räume*, 12.

13. There is evidence that the agora and private buildings were clearly separated; this was less the case with the Roman Forum.

14. Cf. Aristotle, *Politics*, 1274b31–1275b20. W.G. Runciman once observed that we ought to speak of a 'citizen-state', rather than a city state (except that 'state', as I have suggested, can be somewhat misleading).

15. Marx, in his doctoral dissertation, praised Themistocles for persuading the Athenians to found a new Athens on a 'different element', the sea.

16. As Josh Ober has put it, 'the Athenians named their new government "democracy", or *demokratia* in Greek, which combines *demos* ("the people") and *kratos* ("power"). So: democracy is "people power" – but specifically *demos* in the sense of "all citizens", and *kratos* in the sense of "the capacity to do things".' See Josiah Ober, 'The Original Meaning of Democracy', *Constellations*, vol. 15 (2008), 3–9.

17. Plato, *Laws*, ed. Malcolm Schofield (New York, NY: Cambridge University Press, 2016), 641e3 (p. 55).

18. The tribes created by the lawgiver Cleisthenes were precisely not 'tribal' in our colloquial sense; they were highly artificial designs to detach people from local loyalties.

19. Charles Nathan, 'The Urban/Rural Divide in Athenian Political Thought', *American Political Science Review*, vol. 116 (2022), 1, 490–1,502. Distance translated into inequality of participation; it could take up to eleven hours to walk from one of the coastal parts of Attica to the centre of Athens. Eventually, the polis made financial provisions for those losing a day's or two days' work because of the trek to Athens. Paga, *Building Democracy*, 3.

20. Plato, *Laws* 745e (p. 195).

21. Ben Wilson, *Metropolis: A History of a City, Humankind's Greatest Invention* (London: Doubleday, 2020), 80.

22. *Politics* 1331b1 (p. 176), where Aristotle distinguishes a 'freemen's agora' from a 'traders' agora'.

23. Alex Gottesman, *Politics and the Street in Democratic Athens* (Cambridge: Cambridge University Press, 2014), 29.

24. Contrary to legend, the tyranny did not finish with their deed: Hipparchos's brother Hippias took the reins and made

the regime much more oppressive; only four years later was
Hippias forced to leave Athens, under pressure from Sparta.

25. Burkhard Fehr, *Die Tyrannentöter, oder: Kann man der Demokratie
ein Denkmal setzen?* (Frankfurt am Main: Fischer, 1984), 11; see
also Vincent Azoulay, *Les Tyrannicides d'Athènes: Vie et mort de
deux statues* (Paris: Seuil, 2014).

26. See the illuminating chapter, 'The Allure of Harmodius
and Aristogeiton: Public/Private Relations in the Athenian
Democratic Imaginary', in S. Sara Monoson, *Plato's Democratic
Entanglements: Athenian Politics and the Practice of Philosophy*
(Princeton, NJ: Princeton University Press, 2000).

27. Fehr, *Die Tyrannentöter*, 26–7.

28. *Ibid.*, 36–41.

29. Emily Salamanca, 'Pruning of the People: Ostracism
and the Transformation of the Political Space in Ancient
Athens', *Philosophies* (2023), at: https://doi.org/10.3390/
philosophies8050081.

30. There is also evidence that the Lyceum, a venue for sports
exercises and later the site of Aristotle's school, might have
been the initial meeting place of the assembly.

31. Richard Sennett, *Flesh and Stone: The Body and the City in
Western Civilization* (New York: Norton, 1994), 60 and 65.

32. Paga, *Building Democracy*.

33. Of course, there are very real questions as to how much one
would have been able to identify particular others in such large
groups. It is not even clear whether most people were able to
hear the speaker properly. See Christopher Lyle Johnstone,
'Greek Oratorical Settings and the Problem of the Pnyx', in
Christopher Lyle Johnstone (ed.), *Theory, Text, Context: Issues in
Greek Rhetoric and Oratory* (Albany: SUNY Press, 1996), 97–127.

34. 'When many of them sit together in assemblies, courts, theatres,
army camps, or any other gathering of a mass of people in public
and, with a loud uproar, object excessively to some of the things
that are said or done, then approve excessively of others, shouting
and clapping; and when, in addition to these people themselves,

the rocks and the surrounding space itself echo and redouble the uproar of their praise or blame. In a situation like that, how do you think – as the saying goes – a young man's heart is affected? How will whatever sort of private education he received hold up for him, and not get swept away by such praise and blame, and be carried off by the flood wherever it goes, so that he will call the same things beautiful or ugly, as these people, practise what they practise, won't become like them?' Plato, *The Republic*, 492b5–c6 (pp. 185–6).

35. Virginia Hunter, 'Gossip and the Politics of Reputation in Classical Athens', *Phoenix*, vol. 44 (1990), 299–325.

36. The subjects of gossip and judgement were what the Athenians called the 'recognizable ones', elite members who were most visible in the assembly and other institutions. See Gottesman, *Politics and the Street*, 57 and 68, and Kostas Vlassopoulos, 'Free Spaces: Identity, Experience and Democracy in Classical Athens', *Classical Quarterly*, vol. 57 (2007), 33–52.

37. Karl-Joachim Hölkeskamp, *Theater der Macht: Die Inszenierung der Politik in der Römischen Republik* (Munich: C.H. Beck, 2023), 406.

38. As Katherine E. Welsh concludes, 'the architecture of the Roman theater was designed to make the majority of the spectators feel awed – and small'. See 'Art and Architecture in the Roman Republic', in Nathan Rosenstein and Robert Morstein-Marx (eds.), *A Companion to the Roman Republic* (Oxford: Blackwell, 2006), 496–542; here 512. Greek tragedies and comedies – and the City Dionysia in general – were intensely political in subject matter and served as prompts for political discussion among theatre-goers; it is very plausible to see theatre as an integral part of the democracy (and the theatre space as a space for visualizing the polity as a whole: there is some evidence that people were seated in wedges according to tribe, and that office-holders had particular assigned places). See Monoson's chapter 'Citizen as Theatēs (Theater-Goer): Performing Unity, Reciprocity, and Strong-Mindedness at the City Dionysia', in *Plato's Democratic Entanglements*.

39. Egon Flaig, *Die Mehrheitsentscheidung: Entstehung und kulturelle Dynamik* (Paderborn: Schöningh, 2012). To be sure, eventually a secret ballot was introduced; there remains much dispute among historians about how much of a difference this made.

40. Penelope Davies, *Architecture and Politics in Republican Rome* (New York, NY: Cambridge University Press, 2017).

41. Carl Schmitt, *Glossarium* (diary entries), 18 November 1956.

42. This entire paragraph is indebted to Egon Flaig, *Ritualisierte Politik: Zeichen, Gesten und Herrschaft im Alten Rom* (Göttingen: Vandenhoeck & Ruprecht, 2003).

43. See the chapter 'The Augurs and their Spaces', in Daniel J. Gargola, *The Shape of the Roman Order: The Republic and Its Spaces* (Chapel Hill, NC: University of North Carolina Press, 2017), 119–53.

44. Brigitte Sölch, 'Das Forum – nur eine Idee? Versuch einer Problemgeschichte aus kunst- und architekturhistorischer Perspektive', *Mitteilungen der Residenz-Kommission der Akademie der Wissenschaften zu Göttingen: Stadt und Hof*, vol. 6 (2017), 147–58.

45. Joëlle Zask, *Se réunir: Du rôle des places dans la cité* (Paris: Premier Parallèle, 2022), 48–9.

46. David Wiles, *A Short History of Western Performance Space* (Cambridge: Cambridge University Press, 2003), 99.

47. In Rome and Constantinople, palaces were placed next to sports venues – the latter were the place where ruler and people met. Spiro Kostof, *The City Shaped: Urban Patterns and Meanings through History* (London: Thames & Hudson, 1991), 74–5.

48. Quoted in Davies, *Architecture and Politics*, 177.

49. Richard Wittmann, *Architecture, Print Culture and the Public Sphere in Eighteenth-Century France* (London: Routledge, 2007).

50. Quoted in Paulette Singley, *How to Read Architecture: An Introduction to Interpreting the Built Environment* (New York, NY: Routledge, 2019), 24.

51. Christoph Möllers, *Demokratie: Zumutungen und Versprechen* (Berlin: Wagenbach, 2008), 33–4.

52. He added: 'All this, I say, tends to anarchy.' See his *Culture and Anarchy*, ed. Stefan Collini (Cambridge: Cambridge University Press, 2006), 85.

53. Think also of Alexis de Tocqueville's anxieties that the 'formless' element of democracy might overwhelm democratic forms; he stated categorically that 'men living in democratic ages do not readily comprehend the utility of forms' and that 'forms become more necessary in proportion as the government becomes more active and powerful, while private persons are becoming more indolent and feeble'.

54. *The Medium Is the Message* (New York: Random House, 1967), 22.

55. Michael Guerriero, 'Barney Frank's Opinions', *The New Yorker* (9 December 2011), at: http://www.newyorker.com/news/news-desk/the-political-scene-barneys-frank-opinions.

56. Vincent Bevins, *If We Burn: The Mass Protest Decade and the Missing Revolution* (New York, NY: PublicAffairs, 2023).

57. The Public Order Act is at: https://www.legislation.gov.uk/ukpga/2023/15/enacted; the government's attempt to elucidate its terms is at: https://www.gov.uk/government/publications/public-order-bill-overarching-documents/public-order-bill-factsheet; criticism from the UN Commissioner for Human Rights can be found at: https://www.ohchr.org/en/opinion-editorial/2023/05/public-order-act-will-have-chilling-effect-your-civic-freedoms-it-must-be.

58. I owe the formulation of taking a stance needing to take place to the excellent study by Orsolya Salát, *The Right to Freedom of Assembly: A Comparative Study* (Oxford: Hart, 2015).

59. Catie Marron, 'Introduction', in Catie Marron (ed.), *City Squares: Eighteen Writers on the Spirit and Significance of Squares around the World* (New York, NY: Harper, 2016), xi–xiii; here xii.

60. True, acclamation is not suspect as such; people might acclaim a genuinely popular leader: think of the line by the Ecuadorian politician José María Velasco Ibarra: 'Give me a balcony and

I will become president' (in fact, he did become president, no fewer than five times in total from the 1930s to the early 1970s).

61. This was the original insight by Hannah Arendt about the 'iron band' of totalitarianism squeezing people together; it has been elaborated in Miguel Abensour's interpretation of Nazi architecture as aiming at 'compactness'. See Miguel Abensour, *De la Compacité: Architectures et Régimes Totalitaires* (Paris: Sens & Tonka, 1997). These thinkers help us also see that public squares are not somehow anti-totalitarian as such, as Michael Kimmelman once claimed when he wrote: 'The public square has always been synonymous with a society that acknowledges public life and a life in public, which is to say a society distinguishing the individual from the state. There were, strictly speaking, no public squares in ancient Egypt or India or Mesopotamia. There were courts outside temples and royal houses, and some wide processional streets.' See Michael Kimmelman, 'The Craving for Public Squares', at: https://www.nybooks.com/articles/2016/04/07/craving-for-public-squares.

62. Jeremy Waldron, 'What Demonstrations Are, and What Demonstrations Mean', at: https://papers.ssrn.com/sol3/papers.cfm?abstract_id=3664849.

63. Salát, *The Right*, 5.

64. A. Philip Randolph quoted in Lucy G. Barber, *Marching on Washington: The Forging of an American Political Tradition* (Berkeley, CA: University of California Press, 2002), 1. Ever since disputes about the attendance at the Million Man March in 1995, the National Park Service no longer releases numbers (the Park Police had estimated that only 400,000 men had participated; they were promptly accused of racism). See *ibid.*, 226.

65. Charles Tilly, Ernesto Castañeda and Lesley J. Wood, *Social Movements, 1768–2018* (New York, NY: Routledge, 2020).

66. Quoted in David I. Kertzer, *Ritual, Politics, and Power* (New Haven, CT: Yale University Press, 1988), 67.

67. Demonstrations against the far right in Germany were organized under the slogan *Wir sind mehr* ('There are more of us'); the 2004 protests in Ukraine prominently featured the line 'Разом нас багато' ('Together we are many').

68. I owe this observation to Wolfgang Scheppe.

69. David I. Kertzer, *Ritual, Politics, and Power* (New Haven, CT: Yale University Press, 1988), 10.

70. Johann Wolfgang von Goethe, *Italienische Reise*, ed. Christoph Michel (Frankfurt am Main: Insel, 1976), 55.

71. Rousseau also reminded eighteenth-century audiences that the poems of Homer had been 'recited before the Greeks solemnly assembled, not in stalls, on stages and cash in hand, but in the open and before the national body'. See Jean-Jacques Rousseau, 'Considerations on the Government of Poland', in *The Social Contract and Other Later Political Writings*, ed. Victor Gourevitch (Cambridge: Cambridge University Press, 1997), 177–260; here 182. Cf. Karsten Harries: 'There is a continuing need for the creation of festal places on the ground of everyday dwellings, places where individuals come together and affirm themselves as members of the community, as they join in public reenactments of the essential: celebrations of those central aspects of our life that maintain and give meaning to existence. The highest function of architecture remains what it has always been: to invite such festivals.' *The Ethical Function of Architecture* (Cambridge, MA: MIT Press, 1997), 365.

72. William H. Sewell, Jr., 'Historical Events as Transformations of Structures: Inventing Revolution at the Bastille', *Theory and Society*, vol. 25 (1996), 841–81.

73. Juliane Rebentisch, 'Rousseau's Heterotopology of the Theatre', in Erika Fischer-Lichte and Benjamin Wihstutz (eds.), *Performance and the Politics of Space: Theatre and Topology* (New York, NY: Routledge, 2012), 142–65.

74. Barbara Stollberg-Rilinger, *Rituale* (Frankfurt: Campus, 2019).

75. Eric Hobsbawm, *Interesting Times* (New York, NY: Pantheon, 2002), 73.

76. A transcript of his remarks can be found at: https://impose
    magazine.com/bytes/politics/slavoj-zizek-at-occupy-wall-street-
    transcript.

77. W.H. Whyte, *The Social Life of Small Urban Spaces* (New York,
    NY: Project for Public Spaces, 1980), 19.

78. Quoted in Timothy Zick, 'Parades, Picketing, and
    Demonstrations', in Adrienne Stone and Frederick Schauer
    (eds.), *The Oxford Handbook of Freedom of Speech* (New York, NY:
    Oxford University Press, 2021), 369–88; here 387.

79. Elias Canetti, *Masse und Macht* (Frankfurt am Main: Fischer,
    1996 [1960]).

80. This paragraph draws substantially on Rania Magdi Fawzy, 'A
    Tale of Two Squares: Spatial Iconization of the Al Tahrir
    and Rabaa Protests', *Visual Communication*, vol. 20 (2018),
    59–80.

81. Mohamed Samir El-Khatib, 'Tahrir Square as Spectacle: Some
    Exploratory Remarks on Place, Body and Power', *Theatre
    Research International*, vol. 38 (2013), 104–15.

82. Fawzy also observes: 'By adding tents and personal belongings
    protestors made the square look almost private, as if it were
    a home – not a camp for universal sharing . . . but a personal
    move, or relocation, for political reasons.' 'A Tale of Two
    Squares', 72.

83. Keller Easterling, *Extrastatecraft: The Power of Infrastructure
    Space* (New York, NY: Verso, 2014).

84. Quoted in Marci Shore, *The Ukrainian Night* (New Haven, CT:
    Yale University Press, 2017), 44.

85. *Ibid.*

86. Also, one baby was born in Tahrir Square and one wedding
    was celebrated. See W.J.T. Mitchell, 'Image, Space, Revolution:
    The Arts of Occupation', *Critical Inquiry*, vol. 39 (2012), 8–32.

87. See https://www.tate.org.uk/whats-on/tate-britain/mark-
    wallinger-state-britain [last accessed 14 may 2025].

88. 'Mark Wallinger on Brian Haw: "It took a while to earn his
    trust"', *The Guardian* (20 January 2011), at: https://www.

theguardian.com/uk/2011/jun/20/mark-wallinger-recalls-brian-haw.

89. *Ibid.*

90. The movements created in Southern Europe during the Eurocrisis built something like porous camps and forums, as opposed to the fortresses characteristic of protests against neoliberal globalization undertaken by anarchists such as the Black Bloc. The latter were precisely *not* open (be it to those passing by or to journalists, let alone the police); they were also not in city centres. These fortresses were used to prepare confrontations. See the chapter 'The Camp and the Agora' in Paolo Gerbaudo, *The Mask and the Flag: Populism, Citizenism, and Global Protest* (London: Hurst, 2017).

91. Matthias Reiss, 'Introduction', in *The Street as Stage: Protest Marches and Public Rallies since the Nineteenth Century* (Oxford: Oxford University Press, 2007), 1–21; here 3.

92. This presumes, though, that 'free universities' and other encampments really remain free: people must be free to enter; people must be free to leave.

93. Owen and other 'utopian socialists' – Marx and Engels' expression – were promptly ridiculed by Marx and Engels for failing to see the structural contradictions of capitalism and for naively putting their trust in elites under capitalism.

94. Of course, such schematic comparisons are prone to the charge of 'digital dualism' – pretending that there is a complete separation between the internet and what is then often misleadingly called 'the real world' (as if the internet was somehow 'unreal'). See Zeynep Tufekci, *Twitter and Tear Gas: The Power and Fragility of Networked Protest* (New Haven, CT: Yale University Press, 2017), 17.

95. The quote is from (then) Republican House Majority Leader Kevin McCarthy; see 'Trump Says Google Is "Rigged" and Suppresses Conservative News', *The New York Times* (29 August 2018).

96. *Packingham v. North Carolina.*

97. Today they are known as X González – and, it seems fair to say, they have somewhat faded from public life.

98. Of course, there is also the possibility that protestors on streets and squares are not what they seem, but this appears a rather remote possibility. By contrast, there is little doubt that de-legitimating protestors as 'paid-up activists' has become a favourite strategy of authoritarians.

99. Frank Pasquale, *The Blackbox Society: The Secret Algorithms That Control Money and Information* (Cambridge, MA: Harvard University Press, 2015).

100. Tim Wu, 'Machine Speech', *University of Pennsylvania Law Review*, vol. 131 (2013), 1,495–1,533, and Eugene Volokh and Donald M. Falk, 'Google: First Amendment Protection for Search Engine Results', *Journal of Law, Economics & Policy*, vol. 8 (2012), 883–99. According to one study, many people have indeed decided that search engines have authority; more trust them now than traditional professional news organizations. See Alexander Halavais, *Search Engine Society*, 2nd ed. (Cambridge: Polity, 2018), 159.

101. Tufekci, *Twitter and Tear Gas*.

102. Ethan Zuckerman, 'This is so much bigger than Facebook', at: https://www.theatlantic.com/technology/archive/2018/03/data-misuse-bigger-than-facebook/556310/.

103. *McIntyre v. Ohio Elections Commission*, 514 U.S. 334 (1995). See also Geoffroy de Lagasnerie, *L'Art de la révolte: Snowden, Assange, Manning* (Paris: Fayard, 2015), and Tali Hatuka and Eran Toch, 'Being Visible in Public Space: The Normalisation of Asymmetrical Visibility', *Urban Studies*, vol. 54 (2017), 984–98.

104. The court also held that 'On occasion, quite apart from any threat of persecution, an advocate may believe her ideas will be more persuasive if her readers are unaware of her identity. Anonymity thereby provides a way for a writer who may be personally unpopular to ensure that readers will not prejudge her message simply because they do not like its proponent.'

105. Tufekci, *Twitter and Tear Gas*.

106. Andrew Guess *et al.*, 'Avoiding the Echo Chamber about Echo Chambers: Why Selective Exposure to Political News Is Less Prevalent Than You Think', *Knight Foundation White Paper*, available at: https://knightfoundation.org/reports/trust-media-democracy.

107. Bernhard Pörksen, *Die grosse Gereizheit: Wege aus der kollektiven Erregung* (Munich: Hanser, 2018).

108. C. Thi. Nguyen, 'How Twitter Gamifies Communication', in Jennifer Lackey (ed.), *Applied Epistemology* (New York, NY: Oxford University Press, 2021), 410–36.

109. As the writer Jay Caspian King has pointed out, 'social media has undeniably become the public square, but those platforms have actually served to dull dissent and turn legitimate protest into an individualistic meme war in which people pick a side and add to a junk pile of online ephemera'. See 'The Radical Case for Free Speech', *New Yorker* (10 May 2024).

110. Marke Beissinger, *The Revolutionary City: Urbanization and the Global Transformation of Rebellion* (Princeton: Princeton University Press, 2022).

111. David Adjaye, 'Djemaa El-Fnaa, Marrakesh: Engaging with Complexity and Diversity', in Marron (ed.), *City Squares*, 83–9.

112. For theorists like Sitte and Brinckmann, cities had to present a coherent image to someone lingering (Sitte's imperative was *Verweile!*); for modernists like Le Corbusier the point was dynamic movement. See for instance A. E. Brickmann, *Platz und Monument: Untersuchungen zur Geschichte und Ästhetik der Stadtbaukunst in neuerer Zeit* (Berlin: Ernst Wasmuth, 1908).

113. Colin Rowe and Fred Koetter, *Collage City* (Cambridge, MA: MIT Press, 1983), 63–4.

114. Ludger Schwarte, *Philosophie der Architektur* (Munich: Fink, 2019), 172.

115. Quoted in Wolfgang Braunfels, *Urban Design in Western Europe: Regime and Architecture, 900–1900*, trans. Kenneth J. Northcott (Chicago, IL: University of Chicago Press, 1988), 92.

116. Karen A. Franck and Quentin Stevens, *Loose Space: Possibility and Diversity in Urban Life* (Abingdon: Routledge, 2007), and Michael Walzer, 'Public Space: Pleasures and Costs of Urbanity', *Dissent*, vol. 33 (1986).

117. In not so democratic situations it can also help if a square is not surrounded by tall buildings that lend themselves to surveillance or, in the worst case, sniping.

118. Joseph W. Esherick and Jeffrey N. Wasserstrom, 'Acting Out Democracy: Political Theater in Modern China', *The Journal of Asian Studies*, vol. 49 (1990), 835–65, and Baz Kershaw, 'Fighting in the Streets: Dramaturgies of Popular Protest, 1968–1989', *New Theatre Quarterly*, vol. 13 (1997), 255–76.

119. Christopher Alexander (with Sara Ishikawa, Murray Silverstein, Max Jacobson, Ingrid Fiksdah-King, Shlomo Angel), *A Pattern Language: Towns, Buildings, Construction* (Oxford: Oxford University Press, 1977), 310–14.

120. Adam Gopnik, 'Place des Vosges, Paris: A Private Place', in Marron (ed.), *City Squares*, 39–51.

121. According to Baukultur-Bericht Öffentliche Räume 2020/2021 (Bundesstiftung Baukultur), at https://www.bundesstiftung-baukultur.de/fileadmin/files/medien/8349/downloads/bsbk_bkb-20-21.pdf, 96.

122. Henri Lefebvre, *The Urban Revolution*, trans. Robert Bononno (Minneapolis, MN: University of Minnesota Press, 2003), 21.

123. Beissinger, *Revolutionary City*, 248.

124. Quoted in *ibid.*, 33.

125. *Ibid.*, 258.

126. Ari Shavit, 'Rabin Square, Tel Aviv: So Empty, So Loud', in Marron (ed.), *City Squares*, 129–39; here 135–6.

127. Beissinger, *Revolutionary City*, 11.

128. On developments in the UK, see Richard Martin, 'Illiberal Britain', *Verfassungsblog* (29 December 2021), at: https://verfassungsblog.de/illiberal-britain; on Germany, see Clemens Arzt, 'Pro-Palästina als unmittelbare Gefahr?',

Verfassungsblog (23 October 2023), at: https://verfassungsblog.de/pro-palastina-als-unmittelbare-gefahr.

129. Danielle Tartakowsky, *On est là! La manif en crise* (Bordeaux: Éditions de Détour, 2020). Still, the protests eventually petered out; the *gilets jaunes* could not hold roundabouts for a longer period.

130. Jürgen Habermas, *Faktizität und Geltung: Beiträge zur Diskustheorie des Rechts und des demokratischen Rechtsstaats* (Frankfurt am Main: Suhrkamp, 1994).

131. Adam Przeworski, *Democracy and the Market* (New York, NY: Cambridge University Press, 1991).

132. Charles Beitz, *Political Equality* (Princeton, NJ: Princeton University Press, 1989).

133. Christopher Essert, 'The Nature and Value of Public Space (With Some Lessons from the Pandemic)', *Fordham Urban Law Journal*, vol. 50 (2022), 61–103; here 61.

134. Nadia Urbinati, *Representative Democracy: Principles and Genealogy* (Chicago, IL: University of Chicago Press, 2006).

135. Parkinson, *Democracy and Public Space*.

136. U.S. District Court for the District of Columbia – 342 F. Supp. 575 (D.D.C. 1972) (9 May 1972).

137. Möllers, *Demokratie*, 33–4.

138. Philip Manow, 'Demokratie und Architektur', *Merkur*, vol. 69 (2015), 45–52.

139. I owe this example to Danny Abramson.

140. I thank Danny Abramson for pointing out how often post-war 'Government Centers' in the US – modelled on the City Beautiful – featured water and large spaces for traffic, such that people literally could not find any ground to protest.

141. https://www.theguardian.com/cities/2017/sep/26/its-really-shocking-uk-cities-refusing-to-reveal-extent-of-pseudo-public-space.

142. Sarah Schindler, 'The "Publicization" of Private Space', *Iowa Law Review*, vol. 103 (2018), 1,093–1,153.

2. PALACE: HOUSES OF THE PEOPLE, FOR THE PEOPLE, BY THE PEOPLE?

1. For the order 'Make Federal Buildings Beautiful Again' see https://www.federalregister.gov/documents/2020/12/23/2020-28605/promoting-beautiful-federal-civic-architecture.

2. https://trumpwhitehouse.archives.gov/wp-content/uploads/2021/01/The-Presidents-Advisory-1776-Commission-Final-Report.pdf.

3. The critic was Kate Wagner; see her brilliant 'The McMansionization of the White House, or: Regional Car Dealership Rococo: A Treatise', at: https://www.patreon.com/posts/mcmansionization-126873692.

4. See https://www.trump.com/residential-real-estate-portfolio/trump-palace-new-york

5. 'Promoting Beautiful Federal Civic Architecture', at: https://www.whitehouse.gov/presidential-actions/2025/01/promoting-beautiful-federal-civic-architecture.

6. Heinrich Wefing, *Parlamentsarchitektur: Zur Selbstdarstellung der Demokratie in ihren Bauwerken. Eine Untersuchung am Beispiel des Bonner Bundeshauses* (Berlin: Ducker & Humblot, 1995).

7. Innocent Batsani-Ncube, 'Outrage: Chinese Power Play in Malawi', *Architectural Review* (May 2024), at: https://www.architectural-review.com/essays/outrage-chinese-power-play-in-malawi.

8. Wefing, *Kulisse der Macht*, 127. Schneider explained that a Caesar's will to rule expressed itself through wanting the most noble, and the most noble, apart from religion, happened to be art and culture.

9. Of course, for the king, private residence and public function could not really be separated. Kings were dressed by aristocrats in the morning, and they were watched by aristocrats as they consumed their dinners at night. Napoleon, who selectively and carefully revived practices of the *ancien regime*, reinstated the *grand couvert* during his imperial reign.

10. As Tim Wilkinson observes, 'few royal palaces have been built since the bourgeois revolutions. In situations in which monarchies clung to power, as in British India, there were some very late examples of the type: the Viceroy's House in New Delhi, for instance, and the Umaid Bhawan in Jodhpur, constructed between 1929 and 1943. The latter is one of the largest private residences in the world, and is still home to the descendants of the maharajah – although half of it is now a luxury hotel. (Contrariwise, the Heliopolis Palace in a suburb of Cairo started out as 'the most luxurious hotel in Africa', and has since been converted into a presidential palace).' See Tim Wilkinson, 'Typology: Palace', *Architectural Review*, at: https://www.architectural-review.com/essays/typology/typology-palace.

11. 'Architektur verherrlicht etwas (denn sie dauert). Darum kann es Architektur nicht geben, wo nichts zu verherrlichen ist.' This would suggest that architecture is inherently monumental – it perpetuates a memory. That is clearly not true of all buildings (if one accepts a building versus architecture distinction).

12. Habermas, *Faktizität und Geltung*, 607.

13. John Quincy Adams, *Memoirs of John Quincy Adams, Comprising Portions of His Diary from 1795 to 1848*, ed. Charles Francis Adams, 12 vols. (Philadelphia, PA: J.B. Lippincott & Co., 1876), vol. 8, 433. No monuments for John Quincy Adams, but he was the first president to be honoured with a library and had numerous places named after him – indeed, more abstract, though hardly iconoclastic, forms of veneration.

14. Note that monuments do not necessarily have to be monumental. On this complex relationship, see Marisa Anne Bass, *The Monument's End: Public Art and the Modern Republic* (Princeton, NJ: Princeton University Press, 2024).

15. Harold Laswell, the influential American political scientist, built a whole theory around this notion in his very last book: Harold Laswell, with Merritt B. Fox, *The Signature of Power: Buildings, Communication, and Policy* (New Brunswick, NJ: Transaction, 1979).

16. The Palatul Parlamentului also holds the world record as the most expensive administrative building.

17. Alexis de Tocqueville, *Democracy in America*, trans. Arthur Goldhammer (New York, NY: Library of America, 2004), 536.

18. *Ibid.*

19. See Françoise Melonio, 'Tocqueville and the Arts in Democracy', at: https://www.sciencespo.fr/artsetsocietes/en/archives/1832.

20. Sigfried Giedion, 'Nine Points on Monumentality', in *Architecture, You and Me: The Diary of a Development* (Cambridge, MA: Harvard University Press, 1958).

21. Lewis Mumford, 'Monumentalism, Symbolism and Style', *Architectural Review*, vol. 105 (1949), 173–80.

22. *Ibid.*, 179.

23. Michael Z. Wise, *Capital Dilemma: Germany's Search for a New Architecture of Democracy* (Princeton, NJ: Princeton Architectural Press, 1998).

24. Michał Murawski, *The Palace Complex: A Stalinist Skyscraper, Capitalist Warsaw, and a City Transfixed* (Bloomington, IN: Indiana University Press, 2019).

25. Herfried Münkler, 'Sichtbare Macht: Das Reichstagsgebäude als politisches Symbol', in Ansgar Klein *et al.* (eds.), *Kunst, Symbolik und Politik: Die Reichstagsverhüllung als Denkanstoß* (Wiesbaden: VS, 1995), 249–58.

26. I adopt the important distinction between accessing and assessing from Onora O'Neill, 'Media Freedoms and Media Standards', in Nick Couldry, Mirca Madianou, and Amit Pinchevski (eds.), *Ethics of Media* (New York, NY: Palgrave, 2013), 21–38.

27. This whole discussion is greatly indebted to Sebastiano Fabbrini, *The Reluctant Architecture of European Power* (Basel: Birkhäuser, 2025); I have also drawn on Carola Hain, *The Capital of Europe: Architecture and Urban Planning for the European Union* (Westport, CN: Praeger, 2004).

28. Quoted in Hanno-Walter Kruft, *Geschichte der Architekturtheorie: Von der Antike bis zur Gegenwart* (Munich: C.H. Beck, 2004 [1985]), 263.

29. Johann Wolfgang von Goethe, 'Von *deutscher Baukunst* (1772)', in *Goethes Werke*, Hamburger Ausgabe, vol. 12 (Hamburg: Christian Wegner, 1960), 7–15.

30. John Ruskin, *The Seven Lamps of Architecture* chapter 6, paragraph 7.

31. Christian Welzbacher, *Monumente der Macht: Eine politische Architekturgeschichte Deutschlands 1920–1960* (Berlin: Parthas, 2016). Welzbacher writes of a *tektonisierte monumentalisierte Moderne* (142).

32. I am grateful to Erika A. Kiss for this point.

33. Tom Avermaete, 'Balcony', in Rem Koolhaas *et al.*, *Elements of Architecture* (Cologne: Taschen, 2018), 1,073–1,258; here 1,158.

34. Dietmar Schirmer, 'State, Volk, and Monumental Architecture', in Andreas Daum and Christof Mauch (eds.), *Berlin – Washington 1800–2000* (Cambridge: Cambridge University Press, 2005), 127–53; Winfried Nerdinger, 'A Hierarchy of Styles: Architecture between Neoclassicism and Regionalism', in *Art and Power: Europe under the Dictators* (London: Hayward Gallery, 1995).

35. Whether the Nazis really had a 'ruin theory' – anticipating not just war, but their own destruction – remains controversial.

36. He hated it because one could not hide behind it, and it could not last for eternity. See Elias Canetti, 'Hitler, nach Speer', in *Das Gewissen der Worte: Essays* (Munich: Hanser, 1975).

37. Adolf Arndt, *Demokratie als Bauherr*. The German *Öffentlichkeit* does not suggest a particular space in the way that the standard English translation 'public sphere' tends to do.

38. Adenauer wrote to Schwippert on 30 June 1949: 'Am Dienstag hörte ich von Ihren Herren . . . dass beabsichtigt sei, den Nordflügel und den Südflügel ganz aus Glas herzustellen . . . Ich glaube doch, verpflichtet zu sein, Ihnen zu sagen, dass . . . ich die grössten Bedenken dagegen habe. Ich war vor zwei Wochen in Genf in dem Hauptbau von Corbusier, der ganz aus Eisen und Glas hergestellt ist. Das Gebäude ist von außen betrachtet fürchterlich, und der Aufenthalt im

Innern ist im höchsten Masse unerfreulich . . . Es gibt nichts
Ungemütlicheres, fast möchte ich sagen, Unerträglicheres,
als einen Aufenthalt in einem solchen Glaskasten. Die
Lichtverhältnisse sind derart unangenehm und störend, dass
ich mir nicht vorstellen kann, dass ein normaler Mensch
in einem solchen Raum vernünftig denken und sprechen
kann. Ich glaube, Ihnen sagen zu dürfen, dass ein solcher
Bau von der weitaus grössten Mehrzahl der zukünftigen
Abgeordneten des Bundestages und den Vertretern des
Bundesrates rundweg abgelehnt werden wird.' Quoted in
Wefing, *Parlamentsarchitektur*, 115. In fact, there was no League
of Nations building by Corbusier in Geneva; it is unclear what
Adenauer had in mind exactly.

39. Quoted in Thomas L. Schumacher, *Danteum: A Study in the
    Architecture of Literature* (Princeton, NJ: Princeton Architectural
    Press, 1985), 35 (originally in 'Relazione sulla Casa del Fascio',
    Quadrante 35/36 [1936], 6).

40. Kurt W. Forster, 'BAUgedanken und GEDANKENgebäude:
    Terragnis Case del Fascio in Como' in Hermann Hipp and
    Ernst Seidl (eds.), *Architektur als politische Kultur* (Stuttgart:
    Reimer, 1996), 253–71.

41. *Ibid.* Terragni also designed a Danteum that would have
    been placed between Piazza Venezia and the Colosseum; its
    'Paradise' would have featured glass columns and open air.

42. Deborah Ascher Barnstone, *The Transparent State: Architecture
    and Politics in Postwar Germany* (New York, NY: Routledge, 2005).

43. Vanessa Grossman, *A Concrete Alliance: Communism and Modern
    Architecture in Postwar France* (New Haven, CT: Yale University
    Press, 2024), 109.

44. Onora O'Neill, *A Question of Trust* (Cambridge: Cambridge
    University Press, 2002), and C. Thi Nguyen, 'Transparency Is
    Surveillance', *Philosophy and Phenomenological Research*, vol. 105
    (2022), 331–61.

45. Quoted by Adrina Forty, *Words and Buildings: A Vocabulary of Modern
    Architecture* (New York, NY: Thames & Hudson, 2000), 288.

46. Jeffrey T. Schnapp, 'The People's Glass House', *South Central Review*, vol. 25 (2008), 45–56. I am grateful to an audience member at Berkeley for offering the argument about shattering the glass.

47. Lutz Koepnick sees the dome as a 'viewing machine' providing an 'experience of panoptic mastery and scopic plenitude' primarily for tourists. See his excellent 'Redeeming History? Foster's Dome and the Political Aesthetic of the Berlin Republic', *German Studies Review*, vol. 24 (2001), 303–23; here 308.

48. Aneta Vasileva and Emilia Kaleva, 'Absorbing Cold War Heritage: From a Stalinist Skyscraper to a Seat in EU Democracy?', in Sophia Psarra, Uta Staiger, and Claudia Sternberg (eds.), *Parliament Buildings: The Architecture of Politics in Europe* (London: UCL Press, 2023), 250–62, and Michał Murawski and Ben Noble, ' "Make it look more democratic, Mikhail Mikhailovich!" Potemkin Parliamentarism and the Project to Redesign the State Duma', in *ibid.*, 237–49.

49. As Florian Meinel puts it, transparency and fully professional parliamentarism are incompatible. Florian Meinel, *Die Vertrauensfrage: Zur Krise des heutigen Parlamentarismus* (Munich: C.H. Beck, 2019), 42.

50. Colin Rowe and Robert Slutzky, 'Transparency, Literal and Phenomenal', *Perspecta*, vol. 8 (1963), 45–54. Rowe and Slutzky contrast Bauhaus and Garches to underline the difference between the literal and phenomenal notions of transparency; and they enthuse about Le Corbusier's transparency as organization of space in particular: 'Le Corbusier's planes are like knives for the apportionate slicing of space. If we could attribute to space the qualities of water, then his building is like a dam by means of which space is contained, embanked, tunneled, sluiced, and finally spilled into the informal gardens alongside the lake' (54). I am grateful to Erika A. Kiss for drawing my attention to the importance of Kepes's theories and helping me make sense of them.

51. Ernst Kantorowicz, *The King's Two Bodies: A Study in Medieval Political Theology* (Princeton, NJ: Princeton University Press, 2016).

52. Philip Manow, *Im Schatten des Königs: Die politische Anatomie demokratischer Repräsentation* (Frankfurt am Main: Suhrkamp, 2008).

53. Mona Ozouf, *La fête révolutionnaire* (Paris: PUF, 1976), and Rolf Reichardt, *Das Blut der Freiheit: Französische Revolution und demokratische Kultur* (Frankfurt am Main: Fischer, 2002).

54. Reichardt, *Das Blut*.

55. T.J. Clark, *The Absolute Bourgeois: Artists and Politics in France, 1848–1851* (London: Thames and Hudson, 1973), 61 and 25.

56. Albert Boime, 'The Second Republic's Contest for the Figure of the Republic', *Art Bulletin*, vol. 53 (1971), 68–83; Marie-Claude Chaudonneret, *La Figure de la République: Le Concours de 1848* (Paris: 1987).

57. This entire paragraph is based on Welzbacher, *Monumente der Macht*.

58. See Fernando Esposito, 'Beflügelte Bilderfahrzeuge für und wider Krieg und Faschismus', at: https://visual-history.de/2020/05/18/befluegelte-bilderfahrzeuge-fuer-und-wider-krieg-und-faschismus/#_ftn4.

59. See the extraordinary volume *La Mort et les Statues* by Jean Cocteau, with photographs by Pierre Jahan (Paris: Les Éditions de l'Amateur, 2008 [1946]). It depicts the removal and destruction of the statues undesirable under the Vichy regime; the visual of a seated Adolphe Thiers lifted up by crane and suspended in mid-air is particularly remarkable, as are the very last pictures of the reptiles of reaction.

60. I draw here on my *What Is Populism?* (London: Penguin, 2017).

61. There are other, more practical advantages, too. Building projects – including major infrastructure undertakings like Istanbul's new airport – are visible to all; they also, as with China's rapid creation of airports, for instance, seem to prove state capacity as such; and they make it easy to push taxpayer

money (or, in the case of Hungary, EU subsidies) to cronies who can return the favour by buying up TV channels or newspapers critical of the populist ruler.

62. Not for nothing has Balázs Orbán, Viktor Orbán's chief strategist (no relation), declared 'architectural revival' a 'top priority of the Hungarian government'. https://twitter.com/BalazsOrban_HU/status/1637388891182301184?cxt=HHwWgIC8oa6hlrktAAAA. This was re-tweeted by the account Architectural Revival (https://twitter.com/arch_revival), whose motto is 'Beauty and Tradition Matters' [sic!] (apparently grammar does not matter).

63. Melis Konakçi, 'Electoral Consolidation through Islamic Populism and Religious Grievance', at: https://dergipark.org.tr/en/download/article-file/2905863.

64. Jon Mathieson and Tim Verlaan, 'The Far Right's Obsession with Modern Architecture', at: https://failedarchitecture.com/the-far-rights-obsession-with-modern-architecture.

65. Bülent Batuman, *New Islamist Architecture and Urbanism: Negotiating Nation and Islam through Built Environment in Turkey* (New York, NY: Routledge, 2018).

66. Kenneth Frampton, *Modern Architecture: A Critical History* (London: Thames & Hudson, 1992), 50.

67. Example: https://www.berlin.de/ba-charlottenburg-wilmersdorf/aktuelles/pressemitteilungen/2022/pressemitteilung.1179087.php.

68. Chong-Ming Lim, 'Vandalizing Tainted Commemorations', *Philosophy and Public Affairs*, vol. 48 (2020), 185–216.

69. Josh Ellenbogen and Aaron Tugendhaft (eds.), *Idol Anxiety* (Stanford, CA: Stanford University Press, 2011).

70. https://derbevoelkerung.de/webcam.

71. Robert Musil, 'Denkmale [10 Dezember 1927]', in *Gesammelte Werke: Prosa und Stücke, Kleine Prosa, Aphorismen, Autobiographisches, Essays und Reden, Kritik*, ed. Adolf Frisé (Reinbek: Rowohlt, 1978), 604–8. As he put it: 'The most noticeable thing about monuments is that one does not notice them.' (604)

72. There is also the issue that, as Aldo Rossi pointed out, monuments can enable rituals; and rituals affirm the meaning of monuments.

73. Quentin Stevens, Karen A. Franck, and Ruth Fazakerley, 'Counter-Monuments: The Anti-Monumental and the Dialogic', *The Journal of Architecture*, vol. 23 (2018), 718–39.

74. There are also what one might call anti-anti-monuments: an opposition to official commemoration in the vein of the designs that gesture at damage and loss: after the second Iraq war, many citizens in the US started to build their own heroic monuments, because they did not want another Maya Lin-style Vietnam memorial which, in their view, would devalue the sacrifice of the fallen.

75. Of course, there is, to put it mildly, an issue with the promise of individual autonomy for me when a majority decision goes against me. Rousseau thought unanimity the solution; we think that waiting for the next election and influencing people such that the decision goes my way is the best we can do under the circumstances.

76. See https://jochengerz.eu/works/monument-against-fascism.

77. 'Two from Berlin', *New Yorker* (19 October 2003), at: https://www.newyorker.com/magazine/2003/10/27/two-from-berlin.

78. Jonathan Daly, 'Superkilen: Exploring the Human–Nonhuman Relations of Intercultural Encounter', *Journal of Urban Design*, vol. 25 (2020), 65–85.

79. As Superflex explains, '. . . as part of a process that SUPERFLEX calls "extreme participation", five groups travelled with SUPERFLEX to Palestine, Spain, Thailand, Texas and Jamaica in order to acquire five objects of their choice. These have since been installed in the park.' See https://www.superflex.net/works/superkilen.

80. I am indebted to Rasmus Øhlenschlæger for these observations.

81. Holger Kleine, *Raumdramaturgie: Inszenierung und Typologie*

von Innenräumen (Basel: Birkhäuser, 2017), and Christian Borch (ed.), *Architectural Atmospheres* (Basel: Birkhäuser, 2014).

82. Carl Schmitt, *The Crisis of Parliamentary Democracy*, trans. Ellen Kennedy (Cambridge, MA: MIT Press, 1988).

83. Meinel, *Vertrauensfrage*.

84. Schmitt adopted the term – shorthand for the liberal bourgeoisie that made its home in an assembly of notables in the nineteenth century – from the Spanish arch-reactionary Donoso Cortés.

85. A less enthusiastic observer might say that these shapes nicely symbolize the grip that the German car industry has on national politics.

86. Meinel, *Vertrauensfrage*, 48.

87. Murawski and Noble, 'Make it look more democratic, Mikhail Mikhailovich!'

88. The speech can be heard at: https://winstonchurchill.org/resources/speeches/1941-1945-war-leader/a-sense-of-crowd-and-urgency.

89. Some studies suggest, though, that 'co-visibility' – or what I referred to as 'inter-visibility' in ancient Athens – is higher in the House of Commons than the Reichstag. See Sophia Psarra and Gustavo Maldonado Gil, 'The Palace of Westminster and the Reichstag Building: Spatial Form and Political Culture', in Psarra *et al.* (eds.), *Parliament Buildings*, 167–93.

90. Christoph Schönberger, *Auf der Bank: Die Inszenierung der Regierung im Staatstheater des Parlaments* (Munich: C.H. Beck, 2022).

91. English republican James Harrington, who considered Venice an aristocratic commonwealth (as opposed to a proper republic), reported: 'I have seen . . . Venice, and the great council balloting . . . they have nothing to say to their acquaintance . . . not a word spoken in it.' Much later, the art historian Jacob Burckhardt also associated Venice with 'political silence' (as well as immobility).

92. Monique O'Connell, 'Representative Spaces of Republicanism: Constitutional Thinking, Virtue Politics, and Venice's Great Council Hall in Early Modern Europe', *Dunamis* (2024), 66–77, at: https://doi.org/10.1484/M.DUNAMIS–EB.5.137689.

93. Guess *et al.*, 'Avoiding the Echo Chamber about Echo Chambers'. For the notion of 'incitement capitalism', see Quinn Slobodian, 'The False Promise of Enlightenment', *Boston Review* (Summer 2019).

94. Quoted in Eamonn Canniffe, *The Politics of the Piazza: The History and Meaning of the Italian Square* (Farnham: Ashgate, 2008), 102.

95. Stephen Gundle, *Glamour: A History* (Oxford: Oxford University Press, 2009).

96. I thank Dieter Grimm, Andreas Voßkuhle and Gertrude Lübbe-Wolff for discussions of the architecture of the Court and its surroundings.

97. John Parkinson, 'A Cautionary Tale from Australia's Parliament Buildings', at: https://policyoptions.irpp.org/magazines/november-2018/cautionary-tale-australias-parliament-buildings.

98. Mareike Kleine and Samuel Huntington, 'Negotiating with Your Mouth Full: Intergovernmental Negotiations between Transparency and Confidentiality', at: https://link.springer.com/article/10.1007/s11558-024-09572-1.

99. Andrew Borg Wirth and Michael Zerafa, 'Barra (Get Out!): Agency for Public Resistance at the Parliament of Malta', in Psarra *et al.* (eds.), *Parliament Buildings*, 263–73.

100. Louis Kahn, *Essential Texts*, ed. Robert Twombly (New York, NY: Norton, 2003), 203.

101. Miralles was in fact inspired by the idea of a monastery. He claimed that 'We started this project by thinking of our remembrances. Out of that came an image. The most clear image that we had was the idea of a university campus or monastery situation, not a big single building. It is not just what they look like. It is how they feel.' Quoted in John Grindrod, *Iconicon: A Journey around the Landmark Buildings of Contemporary Britain* (London: Faber, 2022), 274.

102. John Parkinson, 'How Legislatures Work – and Should Work – as Public Space', *Democratization*, vol. 20 (2013), 438–55. I am grateful to Pratap Mehta for the point about Delhi.

103. Eva von Redecker, 'Ownership's Shadow: Neoauthoritarianism as Defense of Phantom Possession', *Critical Times*, vol. 3 (2020), 33–67.

104. Women could still be sold in nineteenth-century Britain; see Carole Pateman, *The Sexual Contract* (Stanford, CA: Stanford University Press, 2018).

105. W.E.B. DuBois, *Black Reconstruction in America* (New York, NY: Free Press, 1998).

106. Charlotte Klonk, 'Angriff auf die Architektur der Demokratie: Ähnlichkeiten und Unterschiede zwischen dem Sturm auf Brasília und auf das Kapitol', *VerfBlog*, 2023/1/13, at: https://verfassungsblog.de/angriff-auf-die-architektur-der-demokratie/, DOI: 10.17176/20230114-001655-0.

107. In 2013 protestors had climbed onto the roof of the Brazilian Congress; at that time, the occupation of at least parts of the building could have been read as a democratic occupation of the space (and, yet again, a symbolic putting of the people – some of the people – above their representatives); in 2023 the roof was closed off.

108. Neil Levine, *Modern Architecture: Representation and Reality* (New Haven, CT: Yale University Press, 2009).

109. In any case, the outside and the inside of a Kahn building were often radically different; the inside featured an ambulatory, somewhat similar to Gothic cathedrals, which also allowed people an individual way in, literally and symbolically.

110. Jeremy Waldron, *The Dignity of Legislation* (Cambridge: Cambridge University Press, 1999).

111. As James Poniewozik has put it, Mar-a-Lago could be understood as 'a kind of privatized public sphere, the palace of a CEO-president-king, done up in the opulent dictator-chic favored by Third-World kleptocrats'. James Poniewozik,

Audience of One: Donald Trump, Television, and the Fracturing of America (New York, NY: Liveright, 2019), 130.

112. Schultes and Frank's civic forum building would have featured both a cinema and a museum, and it would have encouraged a sense of 'Hier bin ich Volk, hier darf ich's sein' – roughly translatable as 'Here I can be an ordinary citizen and enjoy myself.' In 2021 the architect and interior designer Holger Kleine, together with his students, presented a plan for a large building matching the height of the Löbe Haus to fill the space; they termed it 'Salons of the Republic'. It would have provided many different spaces for 'debates' of varying intensity, but also a rooftop for 'parties'. It will also never be built, but the text reminded the denizens of German democracy what it might be missing; less obviously, it also showed why here, a mutiuse palace, rather than a street lacking crowds, urgency, and intimacy, might have been the right design choice; it would have brought multiple groups of self-selected citizens close, perhaps uncomfortably close, to the seat of executive power. See Holger Kleine (ed.), *Salons der Republik: Räume für Debatten* (Berlin: Jovis, 2021).

113. Eric Klinenberg, *Palaces for the People* (New York, NY: Crown, 2019). As Klinenberg puts it, 'People forge bonds in places that have healthy social infrastructures – not because they set out to build community, but because when people engage in sustained, recurrent interaction, particularly while doing things they enjoy, relationships inevitably grow', 5.

114. Wilson, *Metropolis*, 102; see also Till van Rahden, *Demokratie: Eine gefährdete Lebensform* (Frankfurt am Main: Campus, 2019).

115. Genet observed more broadly: 'Prison offers the same sense of security to the convict as does a Royal Palace to a King's guest. They are the two buildings constructed with the most faith, those which give the greatest certainty of being what they are – which are what they meant to be, and which remain. The masonry, the materials, the proportions and the architecture are in harmony with a moral unity which makes

these dwellings indestructible so long as the social form of which they are the symbol endures. The prison surrounds me with a perfect guarantee. I am sure that it was constructed for me – along with the Law Court, its annex, its monumental vestibule. Everything therein was designed for me in a spirit of the utmost seriousness. The rigour of the rules, their strictness, their precision are in essence the same as the etiquette of a royal court, as the exquisite and tyrannical politeness of which a guest at that court is the object. The foundations of the palace, like those of the prison, adhere in the fine quality of the stone, in marble stairways, in real gold, in carvings, the rarest in the realm, in the absolute power of their hosts; but they are also similar in that these two structures are one the root and the other the crest of a living system circulating between these two poles which contain it, compress it and which are sheer force.' Quoted in Markus, *Buildings and Power*, 96.

116. Rasmussen, *Experiencing Architecture*.

3. STREET: STREAMING AND BLOCKING

1. Jane Jacobs, *The Death and Life of Great American Cities* (New York, NY: Vintage, 1992), 29.

2. Zask, *Se réunir*. Being on the streets, walking among strangers, can also be per se desirable; anyone doubting that should think back to the COVID lockdowns.

3. Vittorio Magnago Lampugnani, *Bedeutsame Belanglosigkeiten: Kleine Dinge im Stadtraum* (Berlin: Wagenbach, 2023), 222.

4. This riffs on a canonical formulation by Theodor W. Adorno.

5. Dilip Parameshwar Gaonkar, with Charles Taylor and Craig Calhoun, *Degenerations of Democracy* (Cambridge, MA: Harvard University Press, 2022), 206. Emphasis in original.

6. G.W. Allport, *The Nature of Prejudice* (Cambridge, MA: Perseus Books, 1954).

7. Jasmine English and Bernardo Zacka, 'The Politics of Sight', *American Political Science Review*, vol. 116 (2022), 1,025–37.

8. John Dewey, *The Public and Its Problems* (Chicago, IL: Swallow Press, 1954), 213.

9. Jacobs, *Death and Life*, 56.

10. *Ibid.*

11. Klinenberg, *Palaces for the People*.

12. Saul Alinsky, *Rules for Radicals* (New York, NY: Random House, 1971).

13. Walter Benjamin, *Das Passagen-Werk*, ed. Rolf Tiedemann, vol. 2 (Frankfurt am Main: Suhrkamp, 1983), 1,051 and 1,052.

14. Quoted in Sarah Ksiazek, 'Architectural Culture in the Fifties: Louis Kahn and the National Assembly Complex in Dhaka', *Journal of the Society of Architectural Historians*, vol. 52 (1993), 416–35; here, 423.

15. See https://baukulturschweiz.ch/en/case-study/stadtlounge-st-gallen.

16. A precedent was the *rue-galerie* in nineteenth-century socialist housing 'palaces', often inspired by Charles Fourier.

17. This also explains why the Smithsons created duplexes: they were as close as possible to the idea of small houses (in the sky).

18. There is also the older idea of a total separation between circulation for cars and for pedestrians. The architects of London's Barbican estate took members of their client, the Corporation of London, to an original site of such separation so as to make the notion plausible: they visited Venice, with its separation of canal traffic and *fondamente*. See Barnabas Calder, *Raw Concrete: The Beauty of Brutalism* (London: Penguin, 2022), 101.

19. Frampton, *Modern Architecture*, 273.

20. Philip Ursprung, *Architektur der Gegenwart: 1970 bis heute* (Munich: Beck, 2025), 17.

21. Jacobs herself named one exception, a high-rise in New York City, where 'balcony-corridors' had become successful spaces for picnic grounds; see Jacobs, *Death and Life*, 43.

22. Dejan Sudjic, *The Language of Cities* (London: Penguin, 2019), 199.

23. Personal observations.

24. Baukultur-Bericht Öffentliche Räume 2020/2021, 67.
25. Georg Simmel, 'Die Großstädte und das Geistesleben', in Georg Simmel, *Gesamtausgabe*, ed. O. von Rammstedt, vol. 7 (Frankfurt am Main: Suhrkamp, 1995), 116–31, and Richard Sennett, *Building and Dwelling* (New York, NY: FSG, 2018), 28.
26. Simmel also associated the city with the intellect (as opposed to emotion) and the rule of (anonymous) money.
27. Lorca observed: 'The two elements the traveler first captures in the big city are extra human architecture and furious rhythm. Geometry and anguish.'
28. One hypothesis to explain increased speed – it is no more than that – is that wages have increased in cities; time is money and less of it should be spent on getting from A to B on streets. See Arianna Salazar-Miranda *et al.*, 'Shifting Patterns of Social Interaction: Exploring the Social Life of Urban Spaces through A.I.', *NBER Working Paper Series*, at: https://www.nber.org/system/files/working_papers/w33185/w33185.pdf.
29. Leslie Kern, *The Feminist City* (New York, NY: Verso, 2021); *Flâneuse: Women Walk the City in Paris, New York, Tokyo, Venice and London* (London: Chatto & Windus, 2016); Elizabeth Wilson, *The Sphinx in the City: Urban Life, the Control of Disorder, and Women* (Berkeley, CA: University of California Press, 1991).
30. Too much attention to others is one thing; too little is arguably still a manifestation of the underlying norms of the street: passers-by ignoring the homeless (or maybe just an unconscious person, or someone recovering from a night of drinking?) stretched out against a wall is an extreme form of indifference based on convenient ignorance – an indifference that can have deadly consequences.
31. Le Corbusier, *Vers une Architecture* (Paris: Flammarion, 1995), 23; Sudjic, *The Language*, 69; Richard Sennett, *Democracy and Urban Form*, 44. All of this – including the café phobia – had been true of Haussmann's renewal programme in Paris as well.
32. Jacobs, *Death and Life*, 320.
33. *Ibid.*, 35.

34. Iris Marion Young, *Justice and the Politics of Difference* (Princeton, NJ: Princeton University Press, 2012), 227.

35. Andrei Marmor, 'What Is the Right to Privacy?' *Philosophy and Public Affairs*, vol. 43 (2015), 3–26.

36. Lowry Pressley, 'Being Known', *The Point*, issue 9 (2014), at: https://thepointmag.com/criticism/known.

37. Erving Goffman, *Relations in Public* (London: Penguin, 1972).

38. Young, *Justice*.

39. Gottesman, *Politics and the Street*.

40. Sennett, *Building*, 275; Barber, *Marching on Washington*, 5.

41. Joshua Clover, *Riot. Strike. Riot: The New Era of Uprisings* (London: Verso, 2019), 8.

42. William H. Sewell, Jr., 'Space in Contentious Politics', in R.R. Aminzade *et al.* (eds.), *Silence and Voice in the Study of Contentious Politics* (Cambridge: Cambridge University Press, 2001), 51–88.

43. Éric Hazan, *La Barricade: Histoire d'un objet révolutionnaire* (Paris: Autrement, 2019). A minority of scholars argue for a military origin and *barrière* as the main etymological source.

44. Mark Traugott, *The Insurgent Barricade* (Berkeley, CA: University of California Press, 2010).

45. *Ibid.*, 105.

46. Esther de Costa Meyer, *Dividing Paris: Urban Renewal and Social Inequality, 1852–1870* (Princeton, NJ: Princeton University Press, 2022), 36.

47. *Ibid.*, 35.

48. Justinien Tribillon, *The Zone: An Alternative History of Paris* (London: Verso, 2024), 23.

49. Wolfgang Scheppe, 'Gottfried Semper and the Practice of Anarchitecture' (on file with author).

50. According to the philosopher Wolfgang Scheppe, they also inspired twentieth-century avant-garde art: collage and montage are prefigured by the barricade; that appears especially true for works put together from the refuse of bourgeois society. See Phillip Pyle, 'Barrikadenwetter: Image

Acts of Insurgency with Wolfgang Scheppe', 27 November 2023, at: https://032c.com/magazine/barrikadenwetter-image-acts-of-insurgency-with-wolfgang-scheppe.

51. Eduard Bernstein, *Der politische Massenstreik und die politische Lage der Sozialdemokratie in Deutschland* (Breslau: Volkswacht, 1905), 13–15. I am grateful to Peter Giraudo for pointing me to Bernstein's views on the functions of the barricade.

52. Clover, *Riot*.

53. Alexis de Tocqueville, *Souvenirs* (Paris: Gallimard, 1999), 185.

54. *La Commune de Paris 1871* (Ivry-sur-Seine: Les Éditions de l'Atelier, 2021), 576–9.

55. Jason Frank, *The Democratic Sublime: On Aesthetics and Popular Assembly* (New York, NY: Oxford University Press, 2021); the remark about the people-making machine is Alain Corbin's, quoted in Enzo Traverso, *Revolution: An Intellectual History* (New York, NY: Verso, 2024), 191.

56. Beissinger, *Revolutionary City*, 351.

57. Encampments can be protected with barricades, as was the case in Tahrir Square. The initial call for Occupy Wall Street had asked people to 'flood into lower Manhattan, set up tents, kitchens, peaceful barricades . . .'

58. Bryn Stole, 'Glue-ten Tag: Behind the Scenes with Germany's Reviled "Climate-Gluer" Activists', *Salon* (3 February 2023), at: https://slate.com/news-and-politics/2023/02/letzte-generation-last-generation-germany-climate-gluers.html. 'Last Generation' reorganized and changed its name in 2024; it moved away from the emphasis on blocking.

59. I am grateful to Éva Forgács for helping me understand Chashnik's role.

60. Oliver Elser *et al.*, *Protestarchitektur: Barrikaden, Camps, raumgreifende Taktiken 1830–2023* (Zürich: Park Books, 2023), 112.

61. *Ibid.*, 241.

62. These structures are brilliantly analyzed in Nick Newman, *Protest Architecture: Structures of Civil Resistance* (London: RIBA Publishing, 2024).

63. Pyle, 'Barrikadenwetter'.

64. Phil A. Neel, *Hinterland: America's New Landscape of Class and Conflict* (London: Reaktion, 2018).

65. David Bell, 'As France Burns, the Far Right Rises', *Unherd* (3 July 2023), at: https://unherd.com/2023/07/as-france-burns-the-far-right-rises.

66. Kostof, *The City Shaped*, 260. Aristotle held that the grid was preferable in times of peace; small, confusing streets had their uses in times of war. See *Politics*, 1330 b.

67. Sudjic, *The Language*, 70.

68. Kostof, *The City Shaped*, 231.

69. James Scott, *Seeing Like a State: How Certain Schemes to Improve the Human Condition Have Failed* (New Haven, CT: Yale University Press, 1998).

70. John Stuart Mill, 'Thoughts on Parliamentary Reform', *Essays on Politics and Society*, ed. J.M. Robson (Toronto, ON: University of Toronto Press, 1977), 311–39.

71. Bernard Manin, 'Why Open Voting in General Elections Is Undesirable', in Jon Elster (ed.), *Secrecy and Publicity in Votes and Debates* (New York, NY: Cambridge University Press, 2015), 209–14.

72. Arendt, *The Human Condition*, 51. As the historian Sarah Igo points out, 'a postwar house with sufficient privacy was believed to promote "democratic living" by fostering the individuality of each of the family's members: not just that of the man of the house but of his wife and children too'; in fact, 'bedroom privacy' written into new public housing codes then also became normative for the suburbs. See Sarah Igo, *The Known Citizen: A History of Privacy in Modern America* (Cambridge, MA: Harvard University Press, 2018), 111–12.

73. Shoshana Zuboff, *Surveillance Capitalism* (New York, NY: Public Affairs, 2019).

74. Ben Green, *The Smart-Enough City* (Cambridge, MA: MIT Press, 2020).

75. Carissa Véliz, 'In the Privacy of Our Streets', in B.C. Newell, T. Timan and B.-J. Koops (eds.), *Surveillance, Privacy, and Public Space* (London: Routledge, 2018), 16–32.

76. 'Mark Zuckerberg Is Building a New Surveillance State', *The Hill* (10 May 2025), at: https://thehill.com/opinion/5292465-meta-ai-glasses-society-threat.

77. *Ibid.*

78. Salát, *The Right*, 15.

79. Timothy Zick, *Managed Dissent: The Law of Public Protest* (New York, NY: Cambridge University Press, 2023), 4.

80. *Ibid.*, 41.

81. John D. Inazu, *Liberty's Refuge: The Forgotten Freedom of Assembly* (New Haven, CT: Yale University Press, 2012).

82. *Cox v. Louisiana*, 379 U.S. 536 (1965).

83. Timothy Zick, *Speech Out of Doors: Preserving First Amendment Liberties in Public Places* (New York, NY: Cambridge University Press, 2009), 11.

84. *Hague v. Committee for Industrial Organization*, 307 U.S. 496 (1939).

85. I thank Holly Bushman for alerting me to the importance of greens in the American democratic imagination.

86. See https://www.bundesverfassungsgericht.de/SharedDocs/Entscheidungen/EN/2011/02/rs20110222_1bvr069906en.html.

87. *Martin v City of Struthers* (1943).

88. Zick, *Managed Dissent*.

89. This system will also try to fit protest into designated, and usually marginalized, 'free-speech zones' (the flipside of which is making prominent squares speech-free zones), and pursue policies of 'Targeted Protest Regulations'. See *ibid.*

90. Quoted in https://www.designboom.com/art/sarah-ross-archisuits-project-los-angeles-11-03-2022. Ross's website is: https://insecurespaces.net/projects.

91. See https://parametric-architecture.com/anti-anti-hostile-architecture-simple-ways-for-inclusive-design/?srsltid=AfmBO oqfDvjLQ9fR_ui_9FNwrJSvtlN7IqD_lvGVQIt3C3vsS3qu7Dnb.

92. 'Bahrain Shouting in the Dark', Aljazeera English, at: https://www.youtube.com/watch?v=xaTKDMYOBOU.

93. Elena Dorato, *Preventive Urbanism: The Role of Health in Designing Active Cities* (Macerata: Quodlibet, 2020), 76.

94. *Ibid.*, 77.

95. 'City Plan Expert Ends Life by Gas', *The New York Times* (1 June 1936).

96. In fact, the design was also curiously reminiscent of Rem Koolhaas's Prisoners of Architecture.

97. Frampton, *Modern Architecture*, 280.

98. Of course, one could turn the logic around: if there is only one street, one block is very effective.

CODA: SEVEN BUILDING BLOCKS FOR THINKING ABOUT ARCHITECTURE AND DEMOCRACY

1. This formulation is obviously a riff on Marx's 'Eighteenth Brumaire'. I thank Heinrich Geiselberger for suggesting it.

2. In ancient Athens that uncertainty was due to lot; in representative democracies based on universal suffrage, uncertainty is created through free and fair elections.

3. In democracies, procedures can also become subject to conflict and be changed over time; the point is that they should not be amended to favour one person or party. The principles underlying procedures – freedom and equality – are subject to continuous reinterpretation.

4. Alan Balfour, *Creating a Scottish Parliament* (Edinburgh: Finlay Brown, 2005), 30. Enric Miralles wrote on one of his drawings:

> *I imagine that a parliament building*
> *Should be organic like a university campus*
> *A special kind of knowledge*
> *Produces*

Parliament's need to have different
Places where to think
To talk
To walk.

Ibid., 41.

5. This is yet again employing the distinction drawn by Christoph Möllers.

6. Anna Feigenbaum, Fabian Frenzel, and Patrick McCurdy, *Protest Camps* (London: Zed Books, 2013), 4.

7. As Jacques Rancière put it in 'Occupation': 'Protesting in the streets of a city always entails that you use a space devoted to circulation as a metaphor of the "public space" of citizenship. In normal protests, however, this metaphorical use is associated with the notion of movement. Protestors take to the streets and go over them to both make their demands visible and embody the dynamic of their protest. This is a diversion from the normal use of the streets, but this diversion is still in keeping with this normal use (moving), which also means that it remains faithful to a certain distribution of the roles and the places, opposing the walkers who circulate their demands to the sitting authorities to whom those demands are addressed.' See http://www.politicalconcepts.org/occupation-jacques-ranciere.

8. Feigenbaum *et al.*, *Protest Camps*, 5.

9. L.A. Kauffman, *How to Read a Protest: The Art of Organizing and Resistance* (Berkeley, CA: University of California Press, 2018). The March was in fact tightly coordinated with the Kennedy administration. It also sidelined female leaders in the civil-rights movement.

10. Think back to Hobsbawm's observation: you can make all kinds of moves, but, in the end, it's either sex or it isn't (see Chapter 1, p. 26).

11. Note the observation by Rainier de Graaf: 'Public space – and I challenge anyone to come up with a better definition – is

space accessible to all, subject only to common law. The immediate implication of that definition is that public space is a product of the law and not of architecture or urban planning. Public space – even successful public space – has nothing to do with either'; he concludes that 'a product of the law, true public space allowed for an arena to oppose the same law'. See Rainier de Graaf, *Four Walls and a Roof* (Cambridge, MA: Harvard University Press, 2017), 119 and 121.

12. As Michael Walzer put it, 'open-mindedness requires public subsidy'. See his 'Public Space', 474.

13. Radbruch considered the Volk a 'gotische Dom, in dem die Massen einander tragen, indem sie einander widerstreben'. Gustav Radbruch, 'Parteienstaat und Volksgemeinschaft', in A. Kaufmann (ed.), *Gustav Radbruch Gesamtausgabe, Politische Schriften aus der Weimarer Zeit*, vol. 12 (Heidelberg: C.F. Müller, 1993), 94–9; here 99.

14. Plato, *Laws*, 708d.

15. Axel Schultes, 'The New Chancellory', *The Journal of Architecture* (1997), 269–82; here 272. As Beatriz Colomina puts it, 'Architecture is not simply a platform that accommodates the viewing subject. It is a viewing mechanism that produces the subject. It precedes and frames its occupant.'

16. Niklas Maak, *Der Architekt am Strand: Le Corbusier und das Geheimnis der Seeschnecke* (Munich: Hanser, 2010), 120.

17. Buildings that depict but do not fulfil the relevant function: as said multiple times in this book, they kind of lie.

Acknowledgements

Architecture is always political, but not every political theorist is obligated to make pronouncements on it. Entering what is officially a very different academic field carries risks: mistakes will be made; misunderstandings might multiply. If their number has been kept low, it is because of many generous friends and colleagues – and sometimes security guards in a parliament building willing to chat with a stranger – who helped me, and often gently corrected me. All remaining mistakes are my responsibility, of course.

For illuminating conversations, I am much indebted to Joseph Bedford, Danny Abramson, Axel Schultes and Charlotte Frank, Astra Taylor and Wolfgang Scheppe. Thomas Kaup guiding my Berlin seminar around the Bundestag and the Dutch embassy proved a special inspiration; also very inspiring were the far too few encounters with Sebastiano Fabbrini. *Er fehlt.*

I am grateful for those who accompanied me, or in fact helped me find my way around, in places not always easily accessible: Robert Atler, Yiftah Elazar, Felix Gerdes, Marianne Groulez, Hanco Jürgens, Sung-Ho Kim, Helen Lee, Mark Lilla, Vladimir Nicula, Bimal Patel, Nils Schmid, and Yael Sternhell. This isn't the place to reminisce about shared adventures and moments of wonder, but the people named here will know what is meant.

For reading parts of the manuscript and providing critical responses, I thank Danny Abramson, Atticus Carnell, Penelope Davies, Noha El-Mikawy, Harriet Flower, Erika A. Kiss, Nino Luraghi, Pratap Mehta, John Ma, and Vladimir Nicula.

For looking at the whole manuscript and providing feedback, I am very much indebted to Hubertus Breuer, Corey Brettschneider, Eva Forgács, Hannelore Kaup, Mark Lilla, Heidrun Müller, and Balázs Trencsényi.

Special thanks also to those who generously participated in a manuscript workshop at Princeton: Peggy Kohn, Spyros Papapetros, Till van Rahden, Heinrich Wefing, Bernardo Zacka. Till has also been a constant source of stimulating materials over the years.

Felix Yiu provided valuable research assistance at an early stage; Holly Bushman's assistance was of immense help once the book began to take shape.

My editors deserve special acknowledgement for exceptionally valuable input over many years: Casiana Ionita, Heinrich Geiselberger, Rasmus Øhlenschlæger and Amélie Petit. Particular thanks to Amélie for memorable explorations of Noisy-le-Grand (about which I hope to write on another occasion). Many thanks also to my copy-editor Richard Mason for very careful engagement with the manuscript.

This book draws on arguments initially developed in 'A Short History of the Roadblock', *Architectural Review* (2024); 'On the Square', *Philosophy and Social Criticism* (2024); 'Palaces for the People: How and of What Should Public Buildings Persuade Citizens in a Democracy?', in: Giuseppe Ballacci and Rob Goodman (eds.), *Populism, Demagoguery, and Rhetoric in Historical Perspective* (Oxford University Press, 2024); 'Streaming and Blocking', *Contemporary Political Theory* (2024); 'Architecture and Democracy', in: Duncan Bell and Bernardo Zacka (eds.), *Architecture and Political Theory* (Bloomsbury, 2020); and 'What Spaces Does Democracy Need', in: *Soundings: An Interdisciplinary Journal* (2019).

Princeton University generously financed much of the research for this book. Two other institutions were also of significant help: the Wissenschaftskolleg zu Berlin and the New Institute, Hamburg; in both institutes, librarians proved exceptionally supportive.

ACKNOWLEDGEMENTS

There are building blocks, and there are foundations. Sarah Chalfant's confidence and sage advice were foundational, as was Erika A. Kiss's unique mixture of passion and scepticism.

I first met László Rajk in his studio in Paulay Ede utca during the summer of 2013, when work on this book had just begun. László was an architect, a film architect, a stage designer, a teacher, dissident, a politician, and still many other things. And he was a uniquely inspiring presence. This book is dedicated to his memory.

Index

Page references in *italics* indicate images.